DAVID BOWIE

ON STAGE IN HOLLAND

THE DUTCH CONCERTS 1987 - 1997
PICTURED BY BERNARD RÜBSAMEN

GLASS SPIDER TOUR

PRESS CONFERENCE PARADISO AMSTERDAM, 30 MARCH 1987

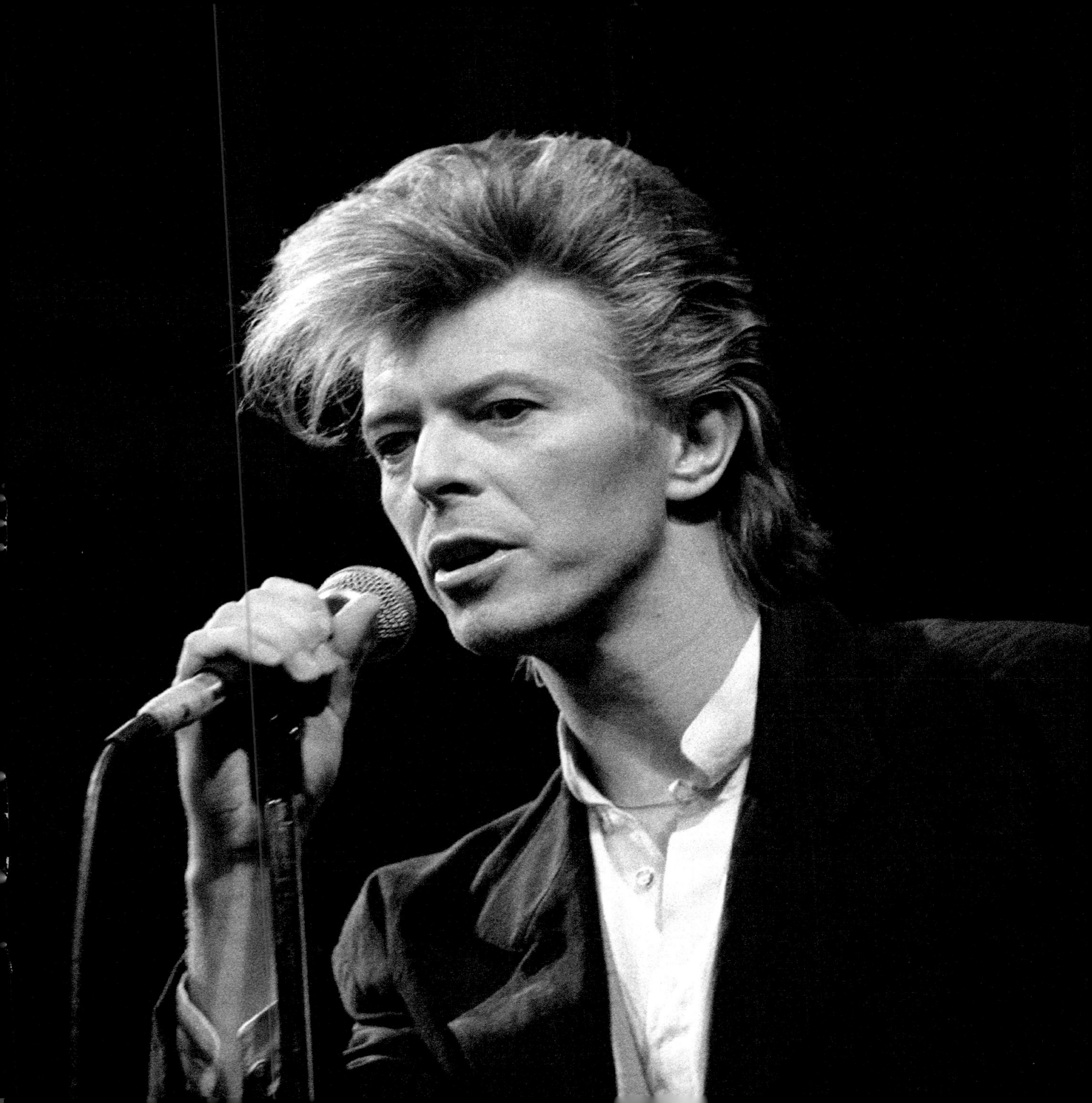

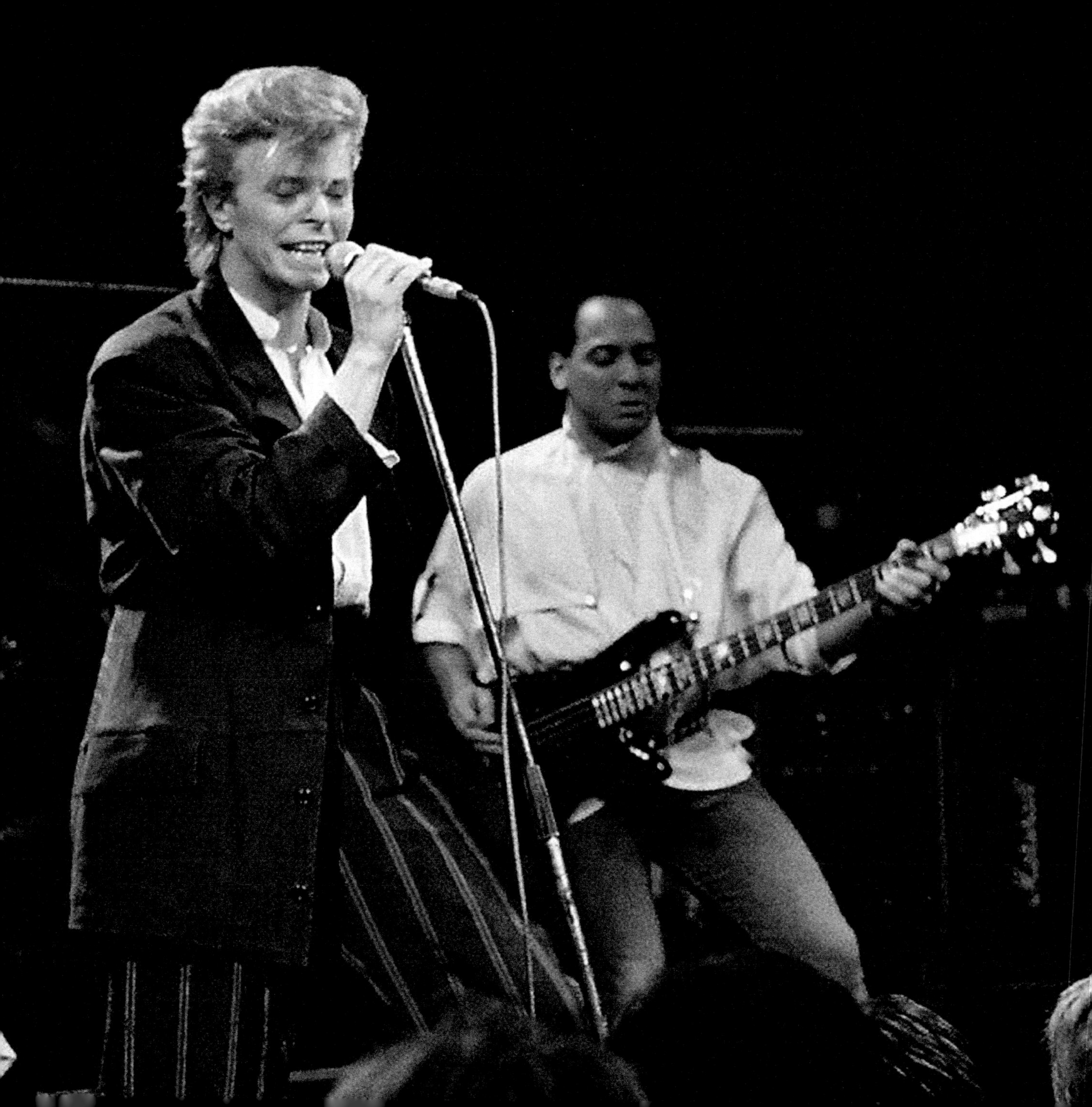

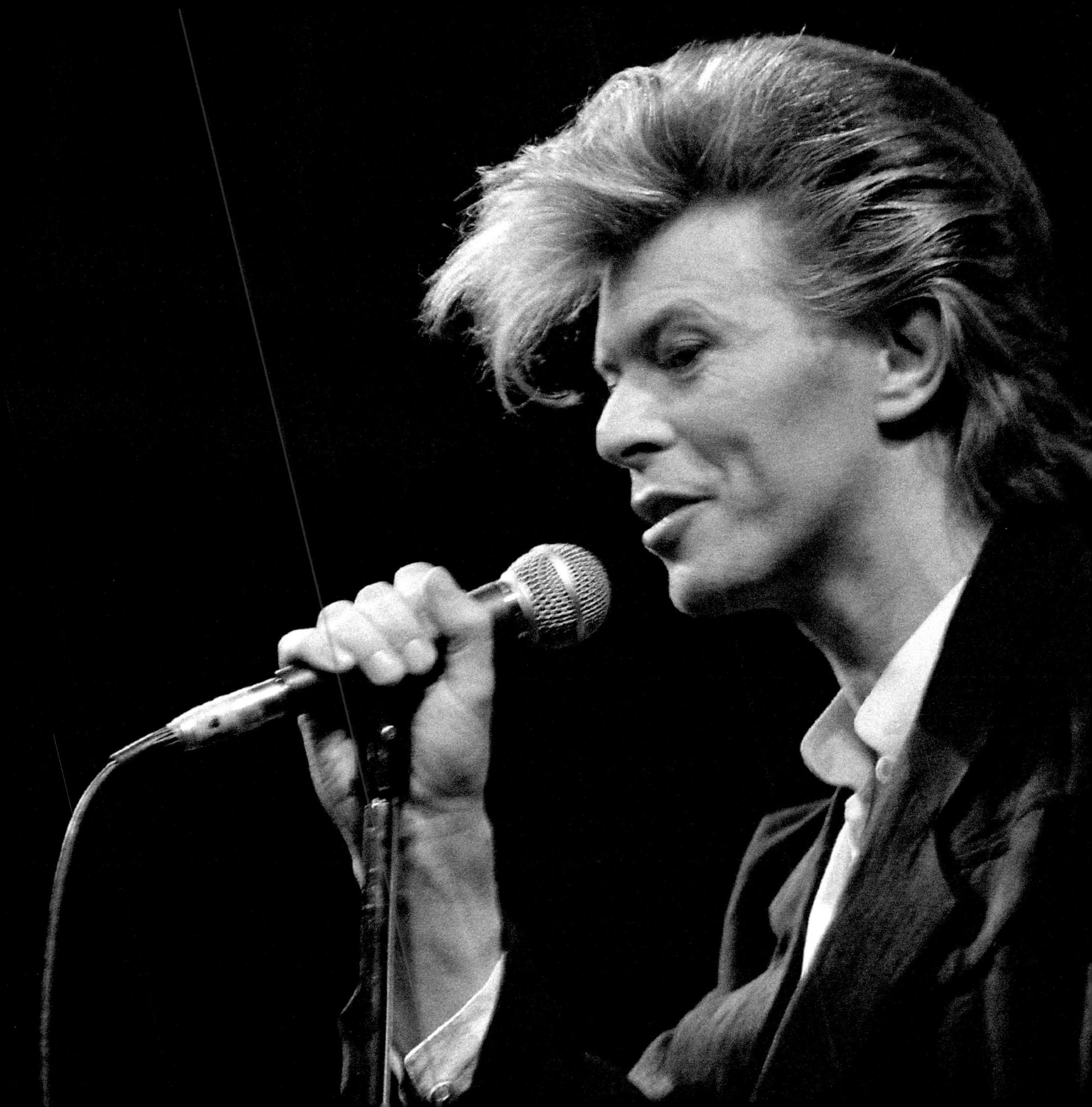

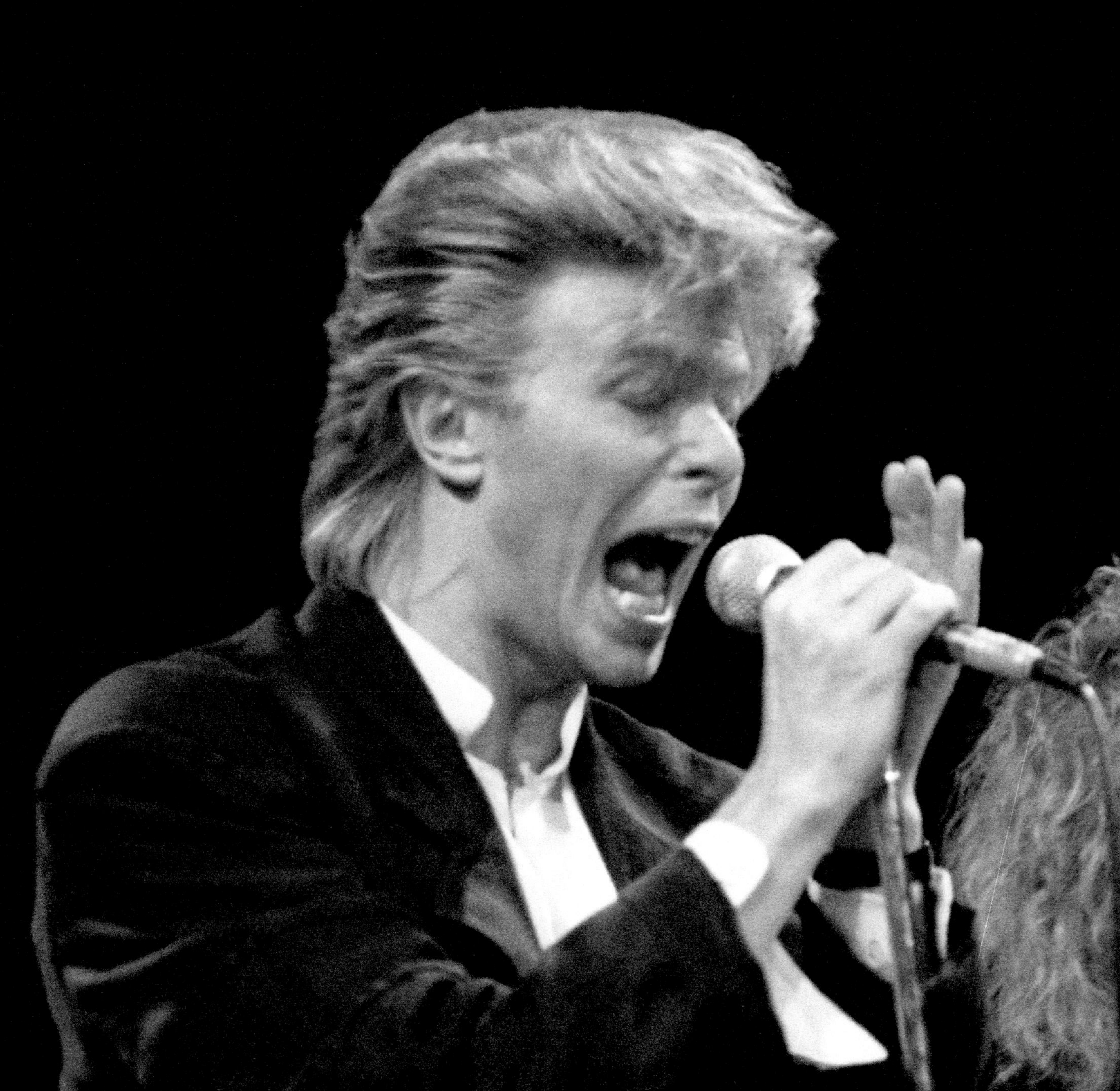

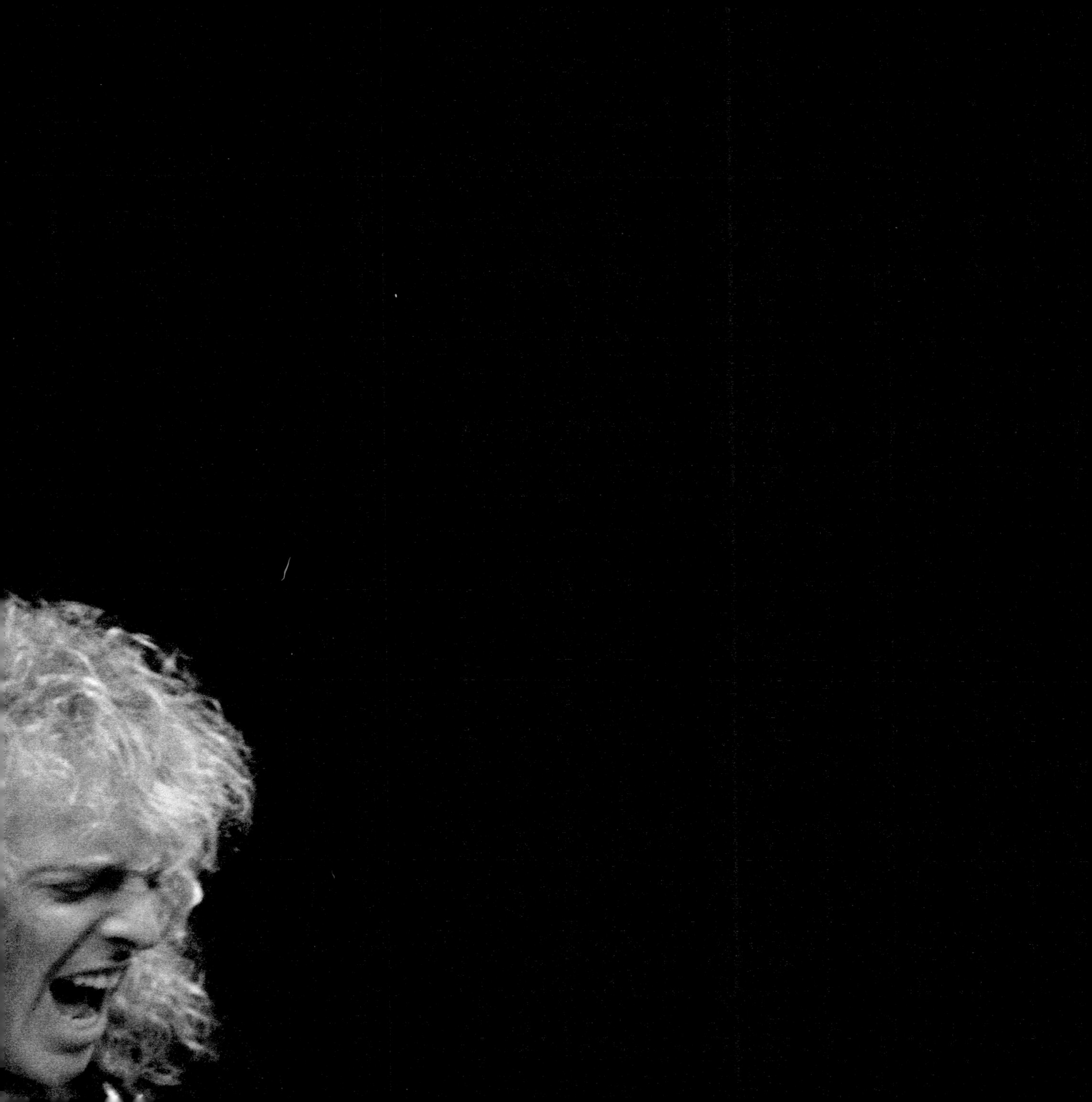

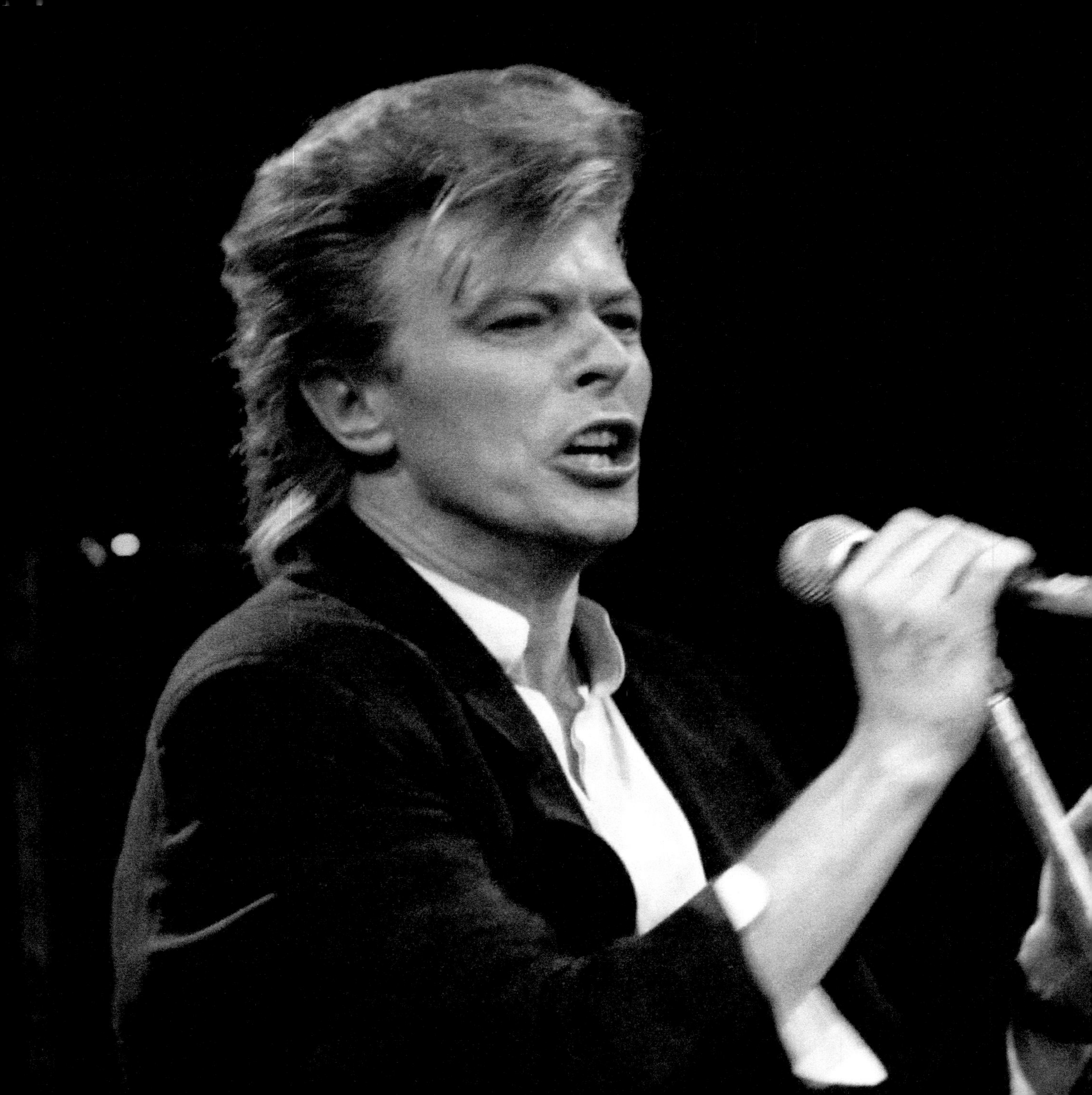

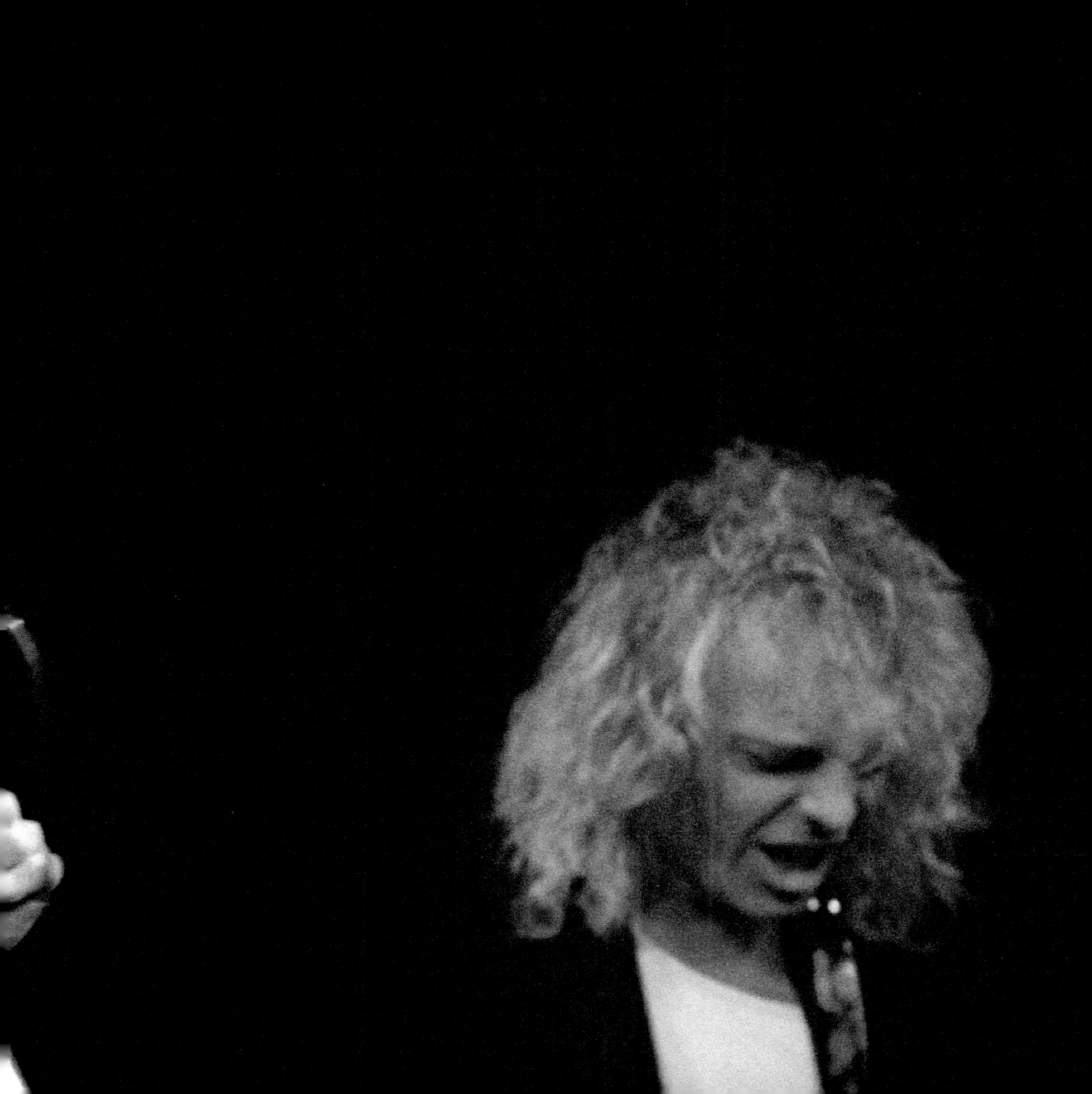

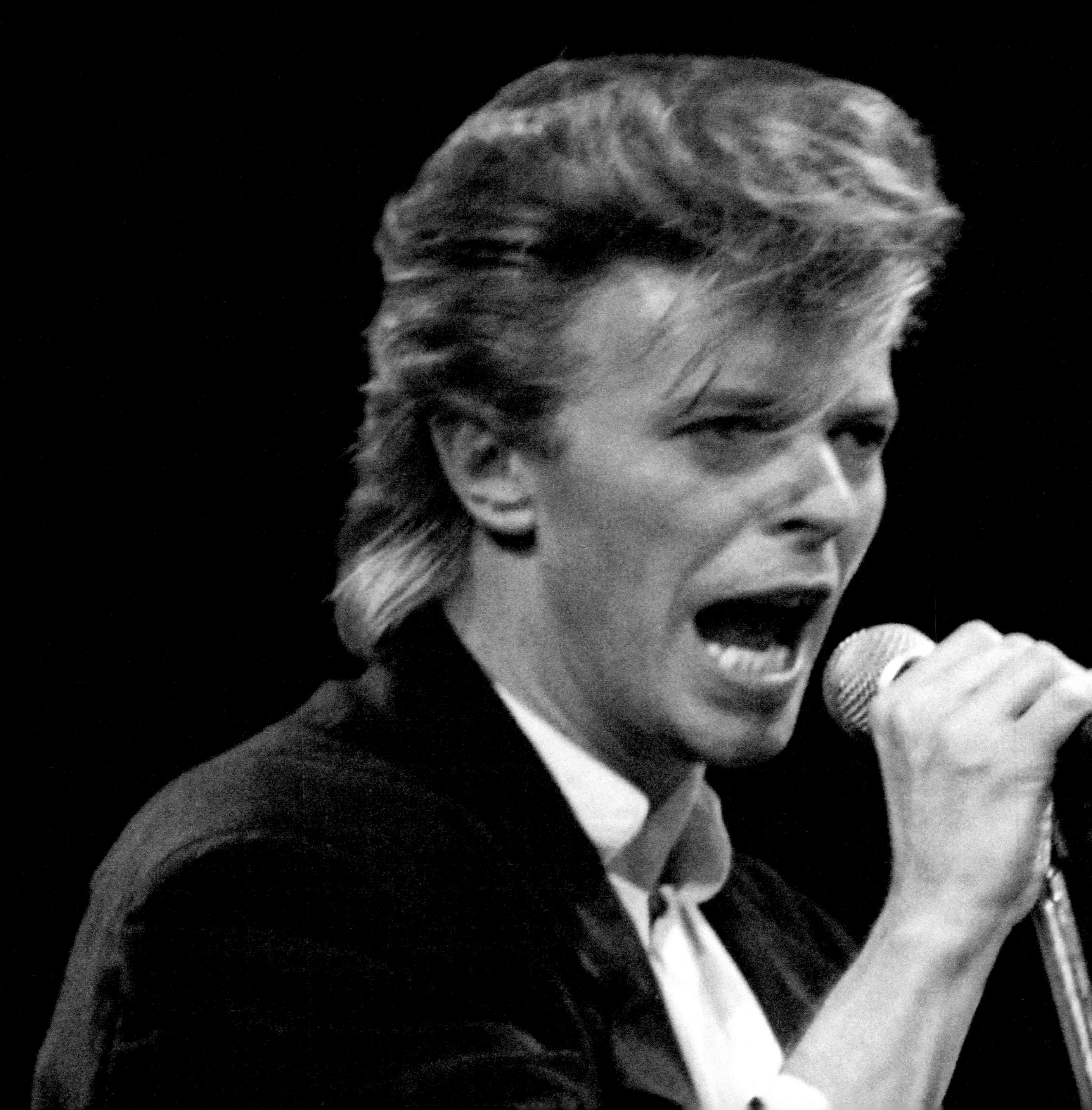

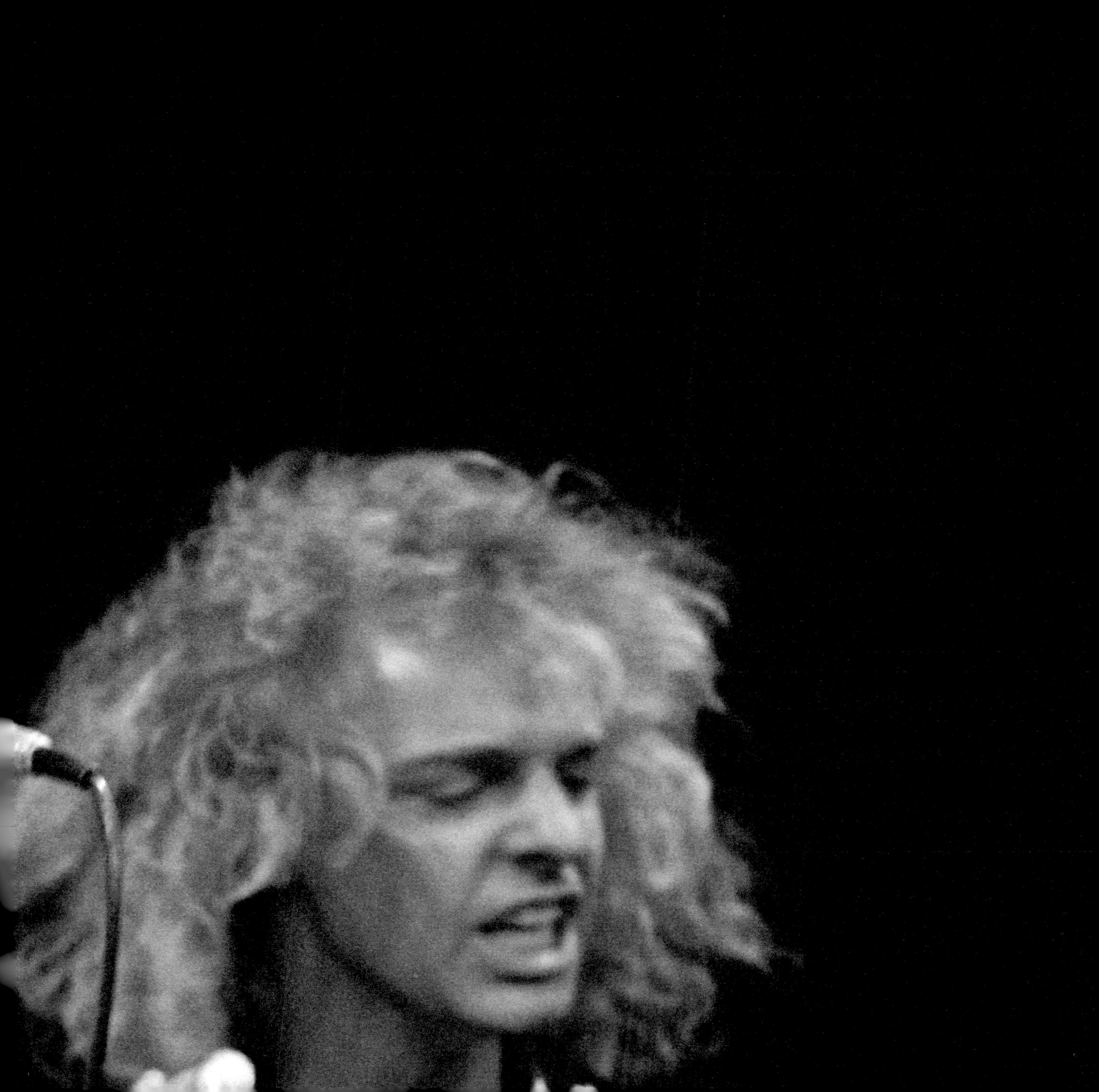

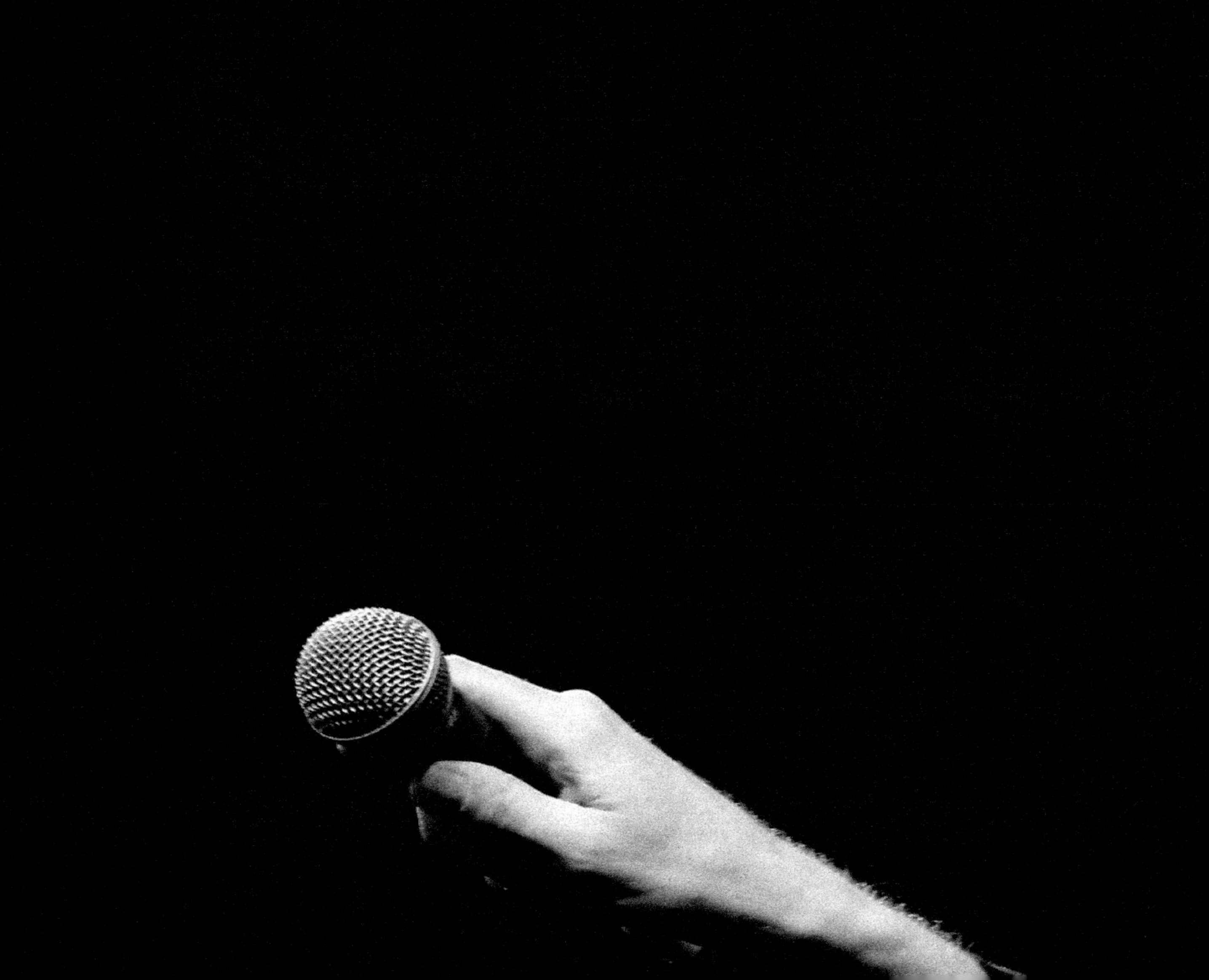

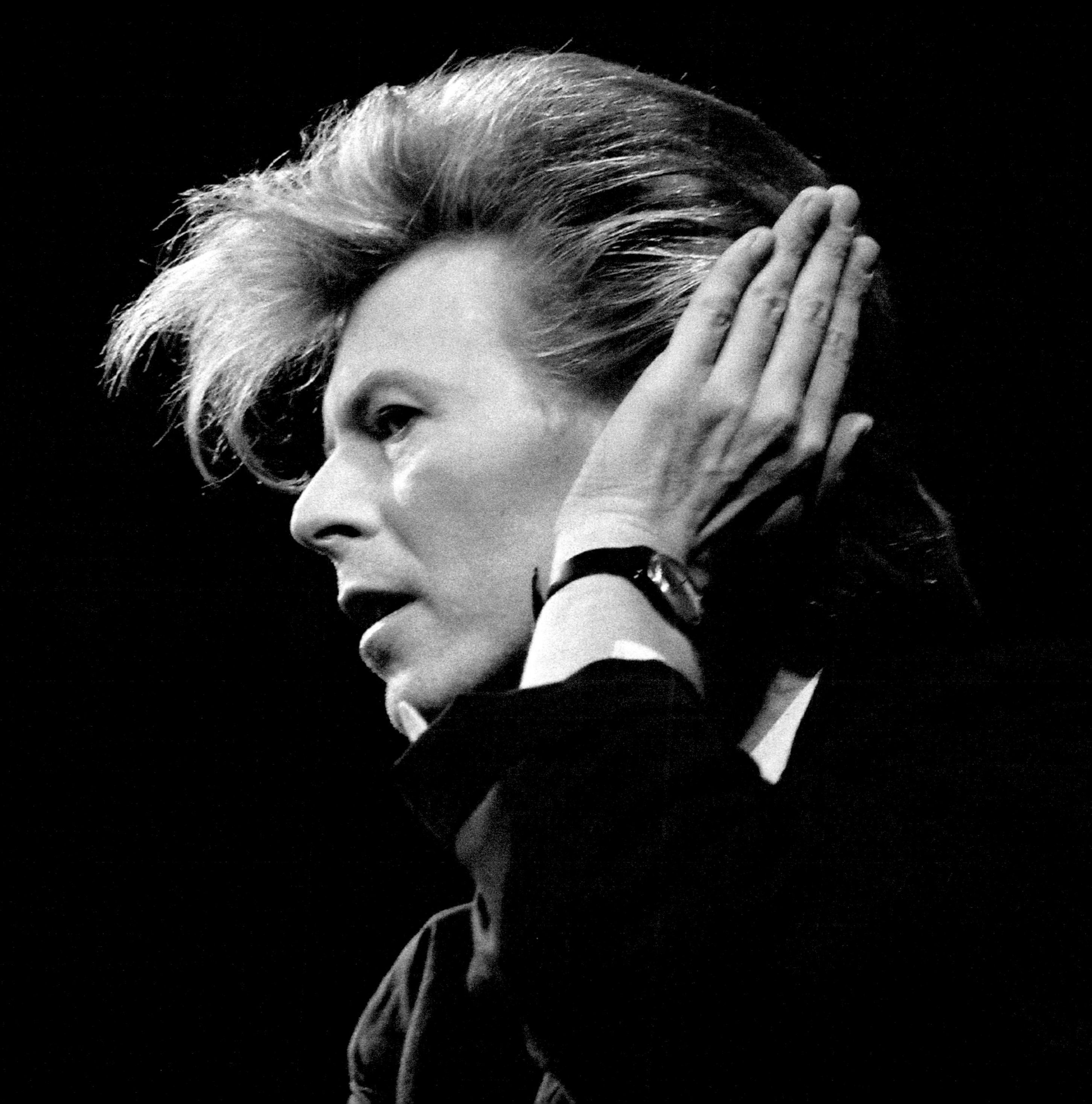

GLASS SPIDER TOUR

STATION FEIJENOORD ROTTERDAM, 30 MAY 1987

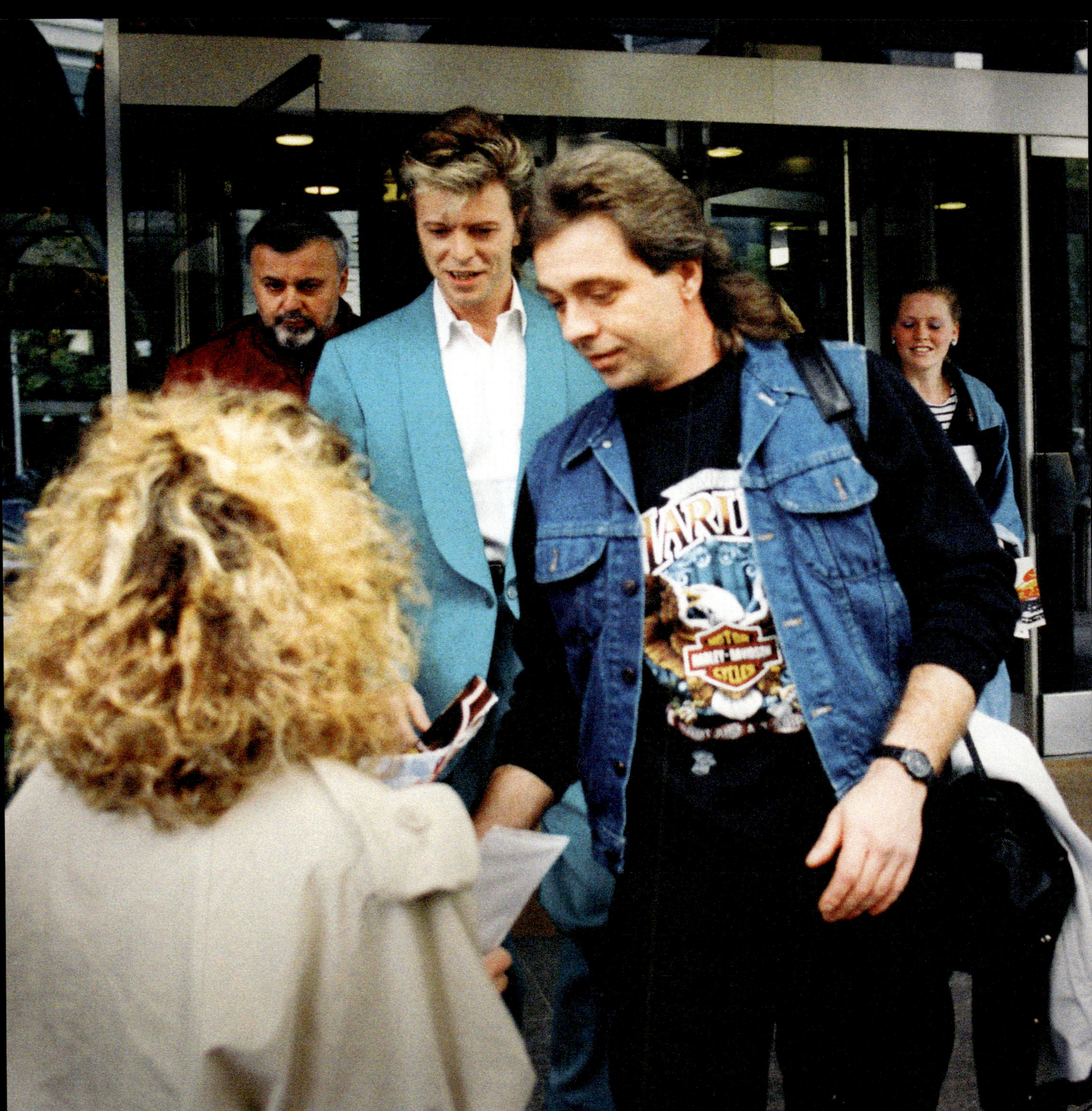

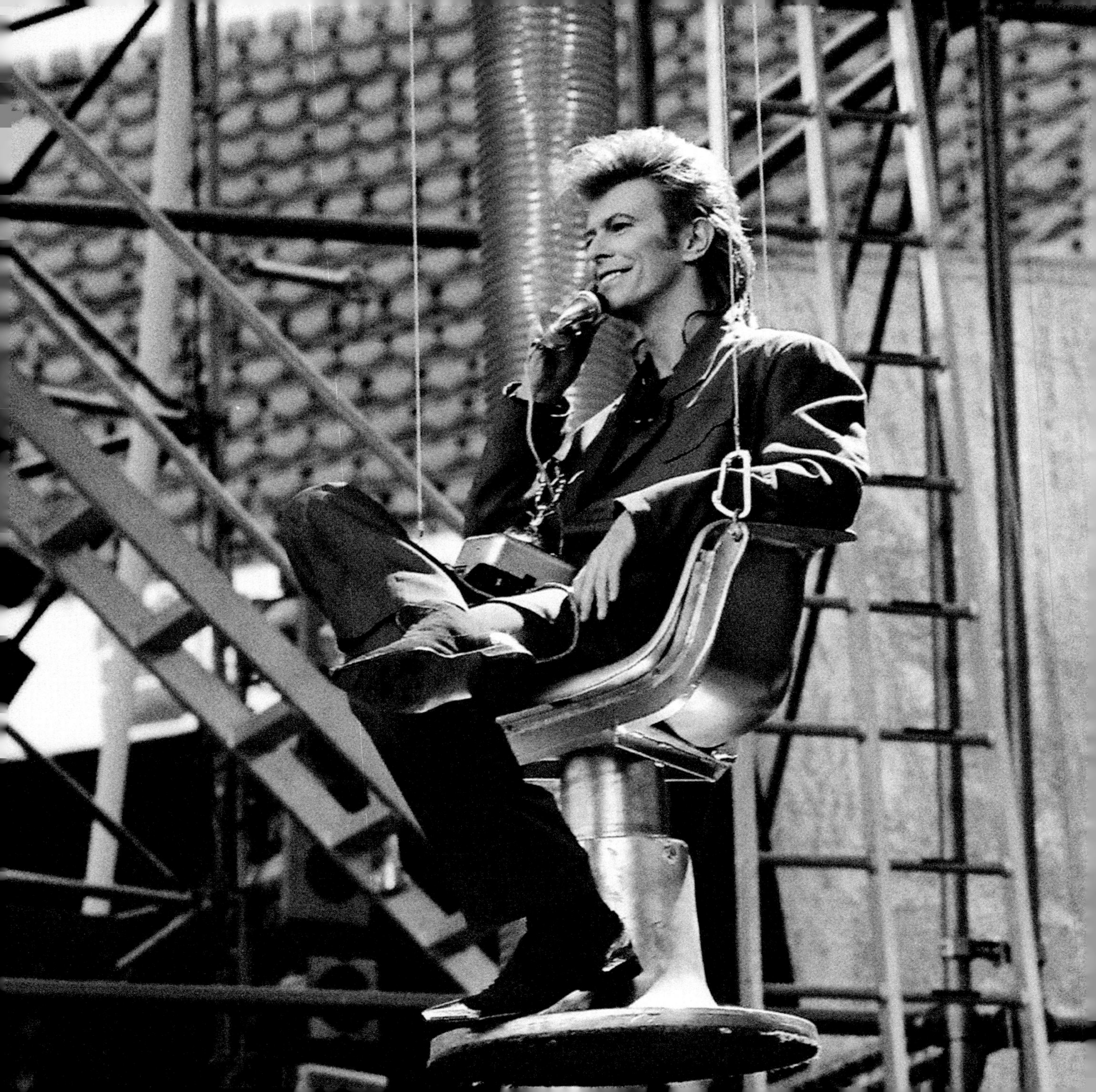

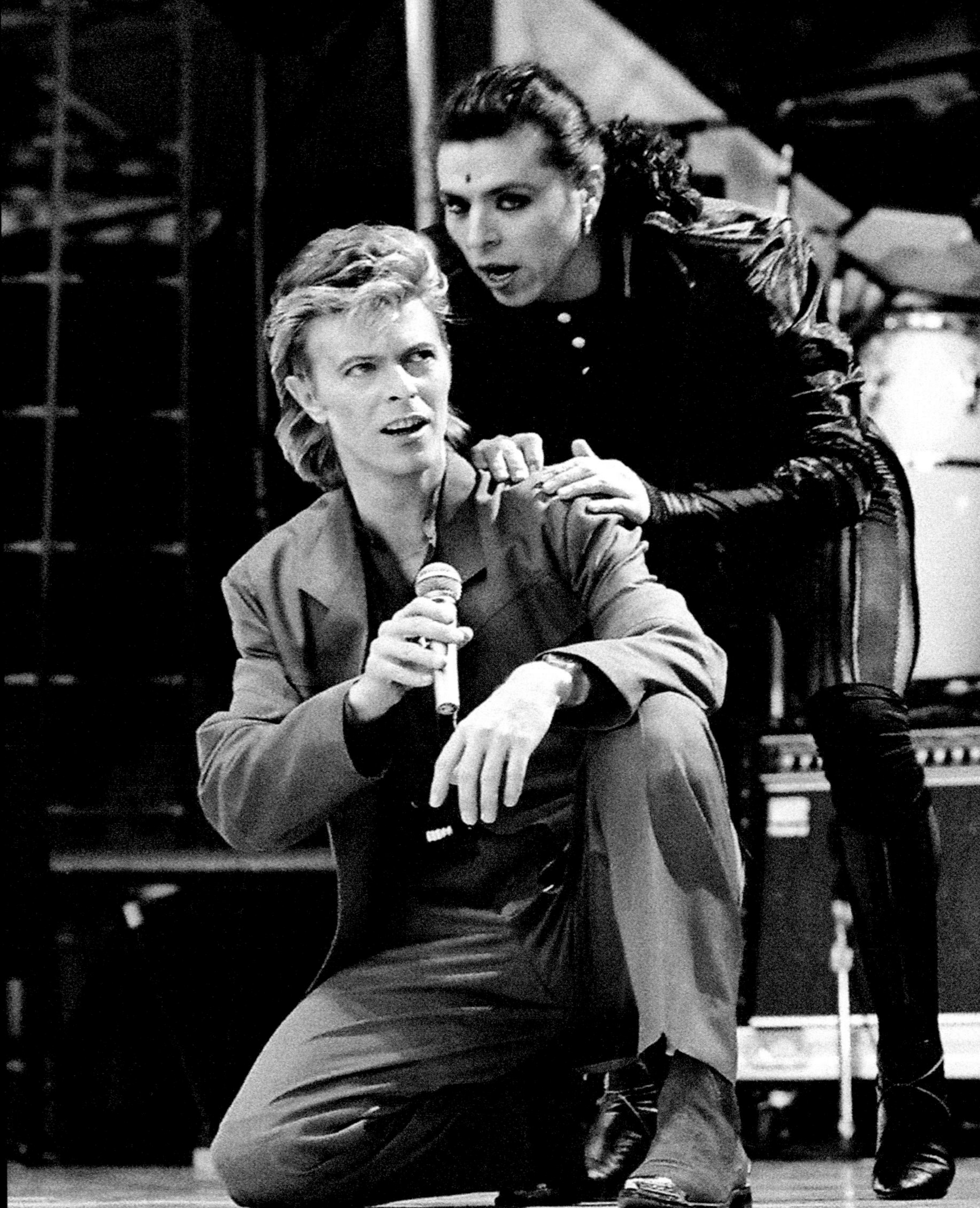

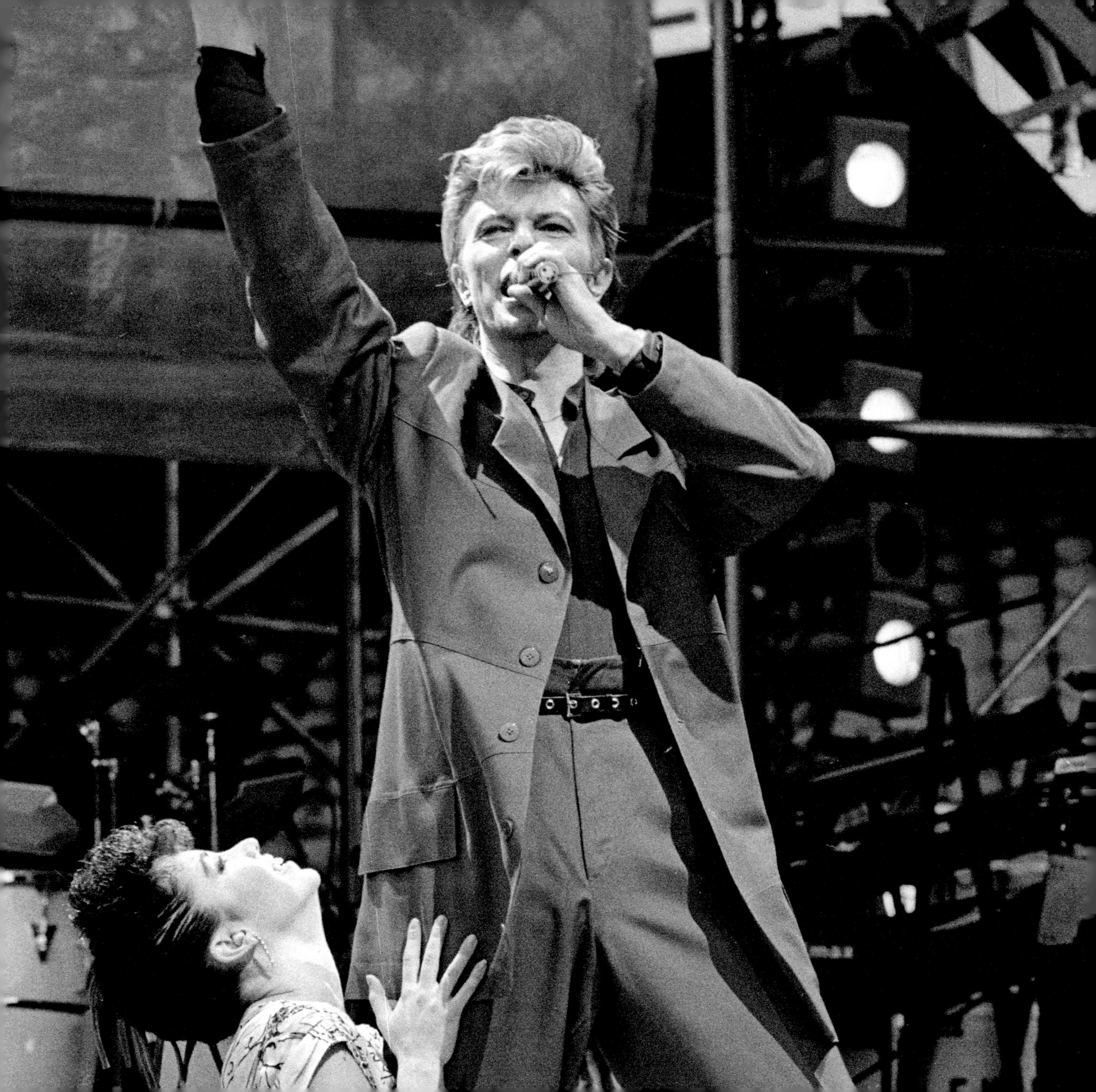

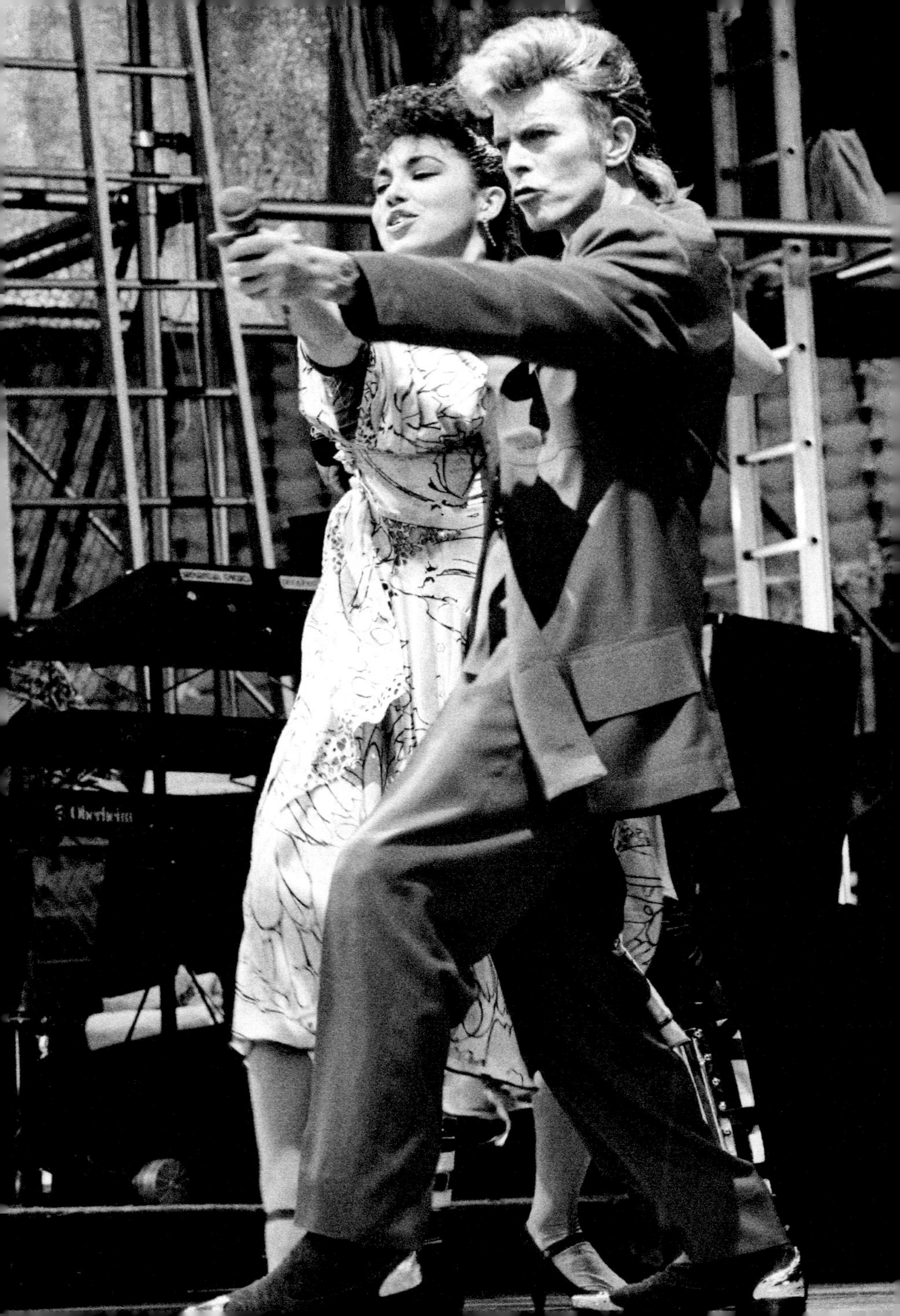
Oberheim

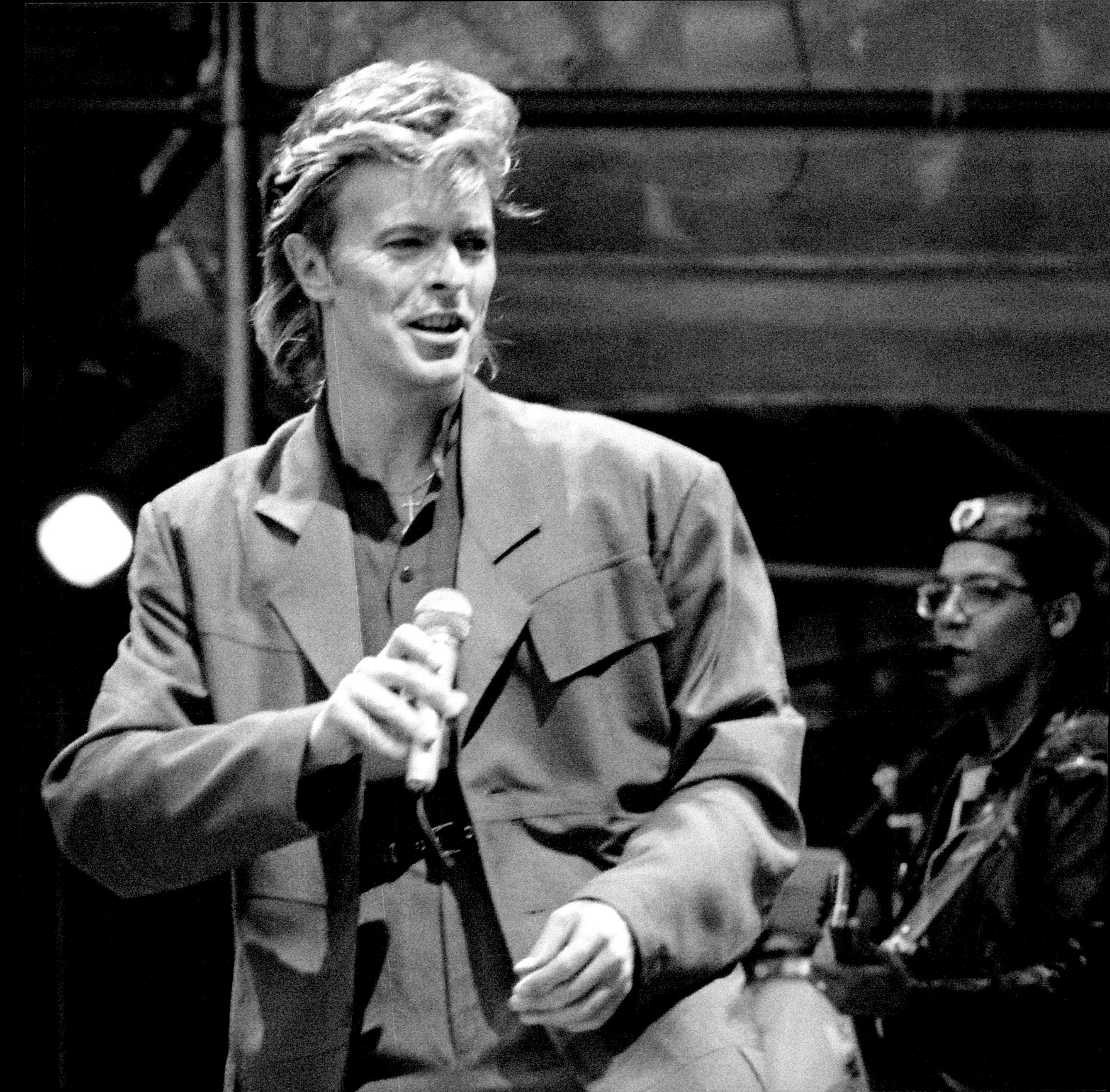

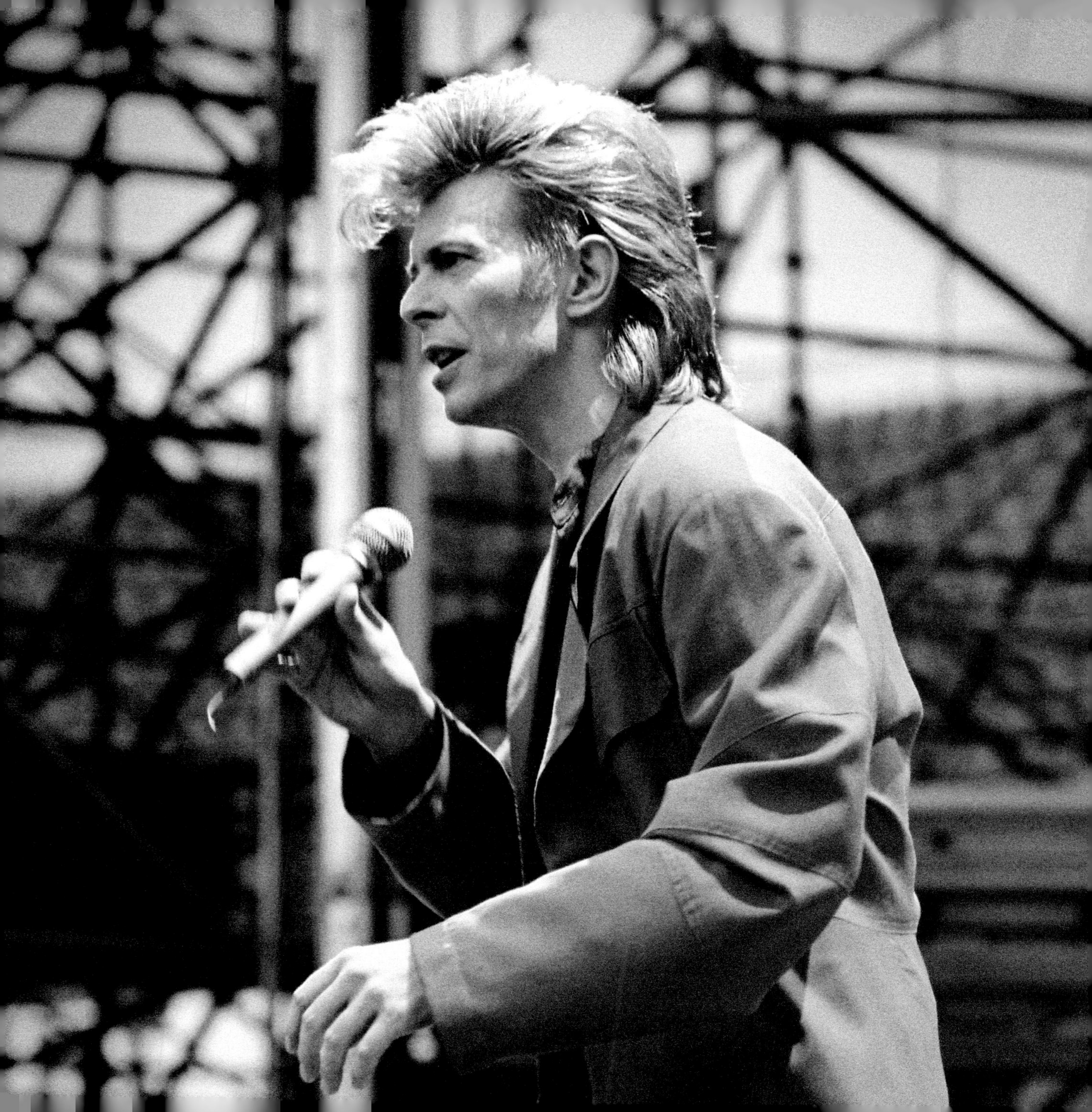

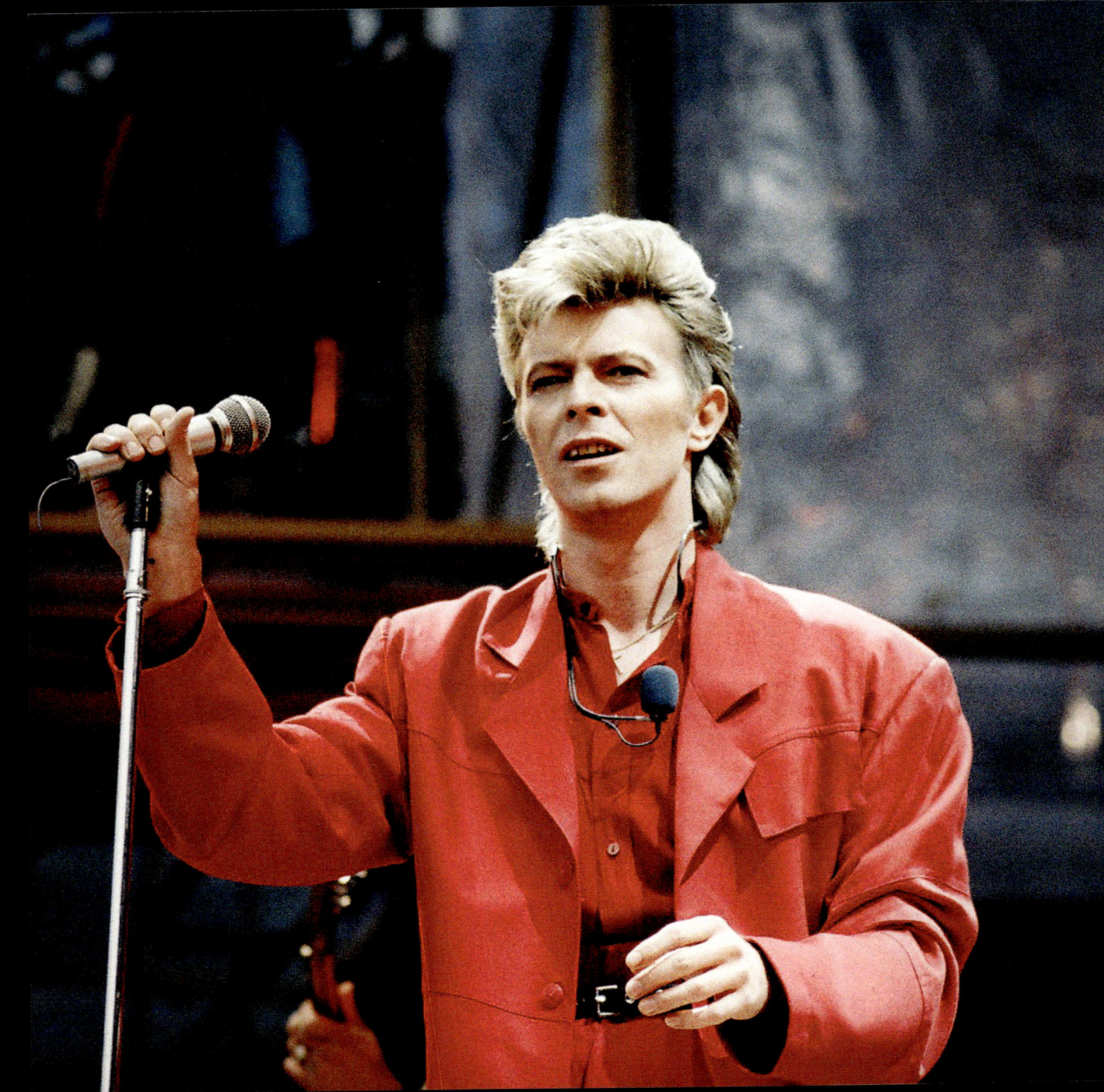

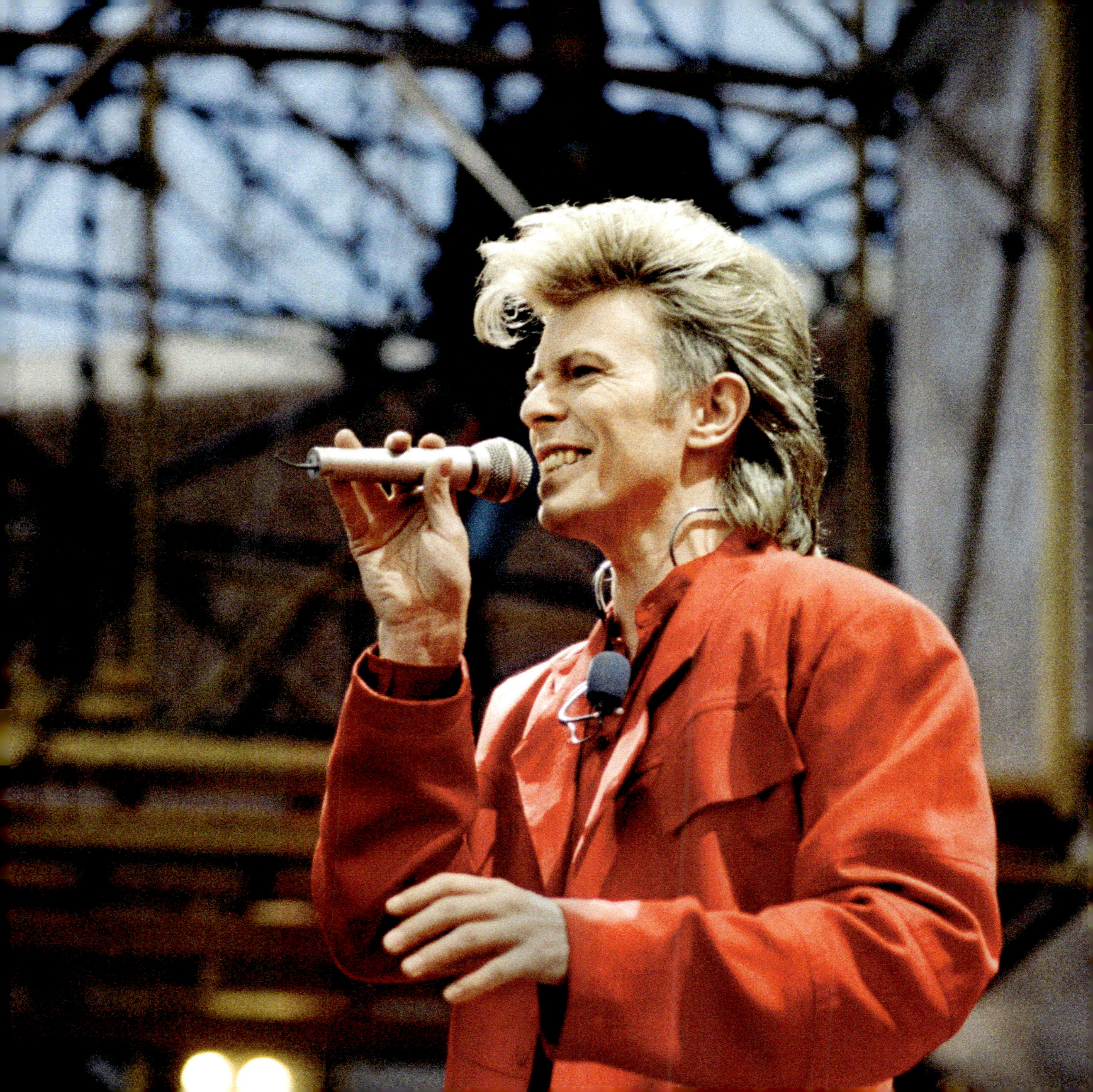

SOUND AND VISION TOUR

SPORTPALEIS AHOY ROTTERDAM, 30 MARCH 1990

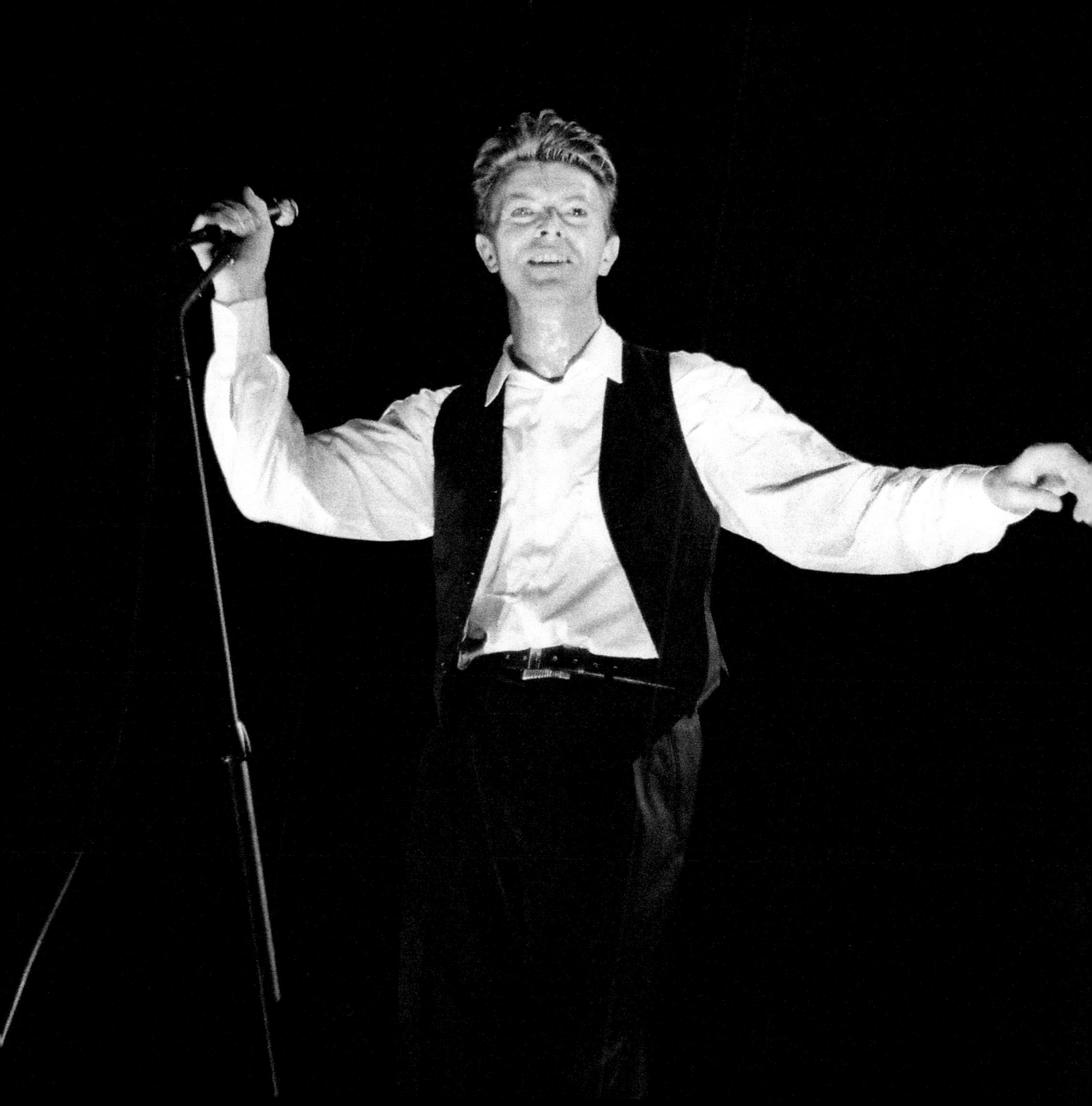

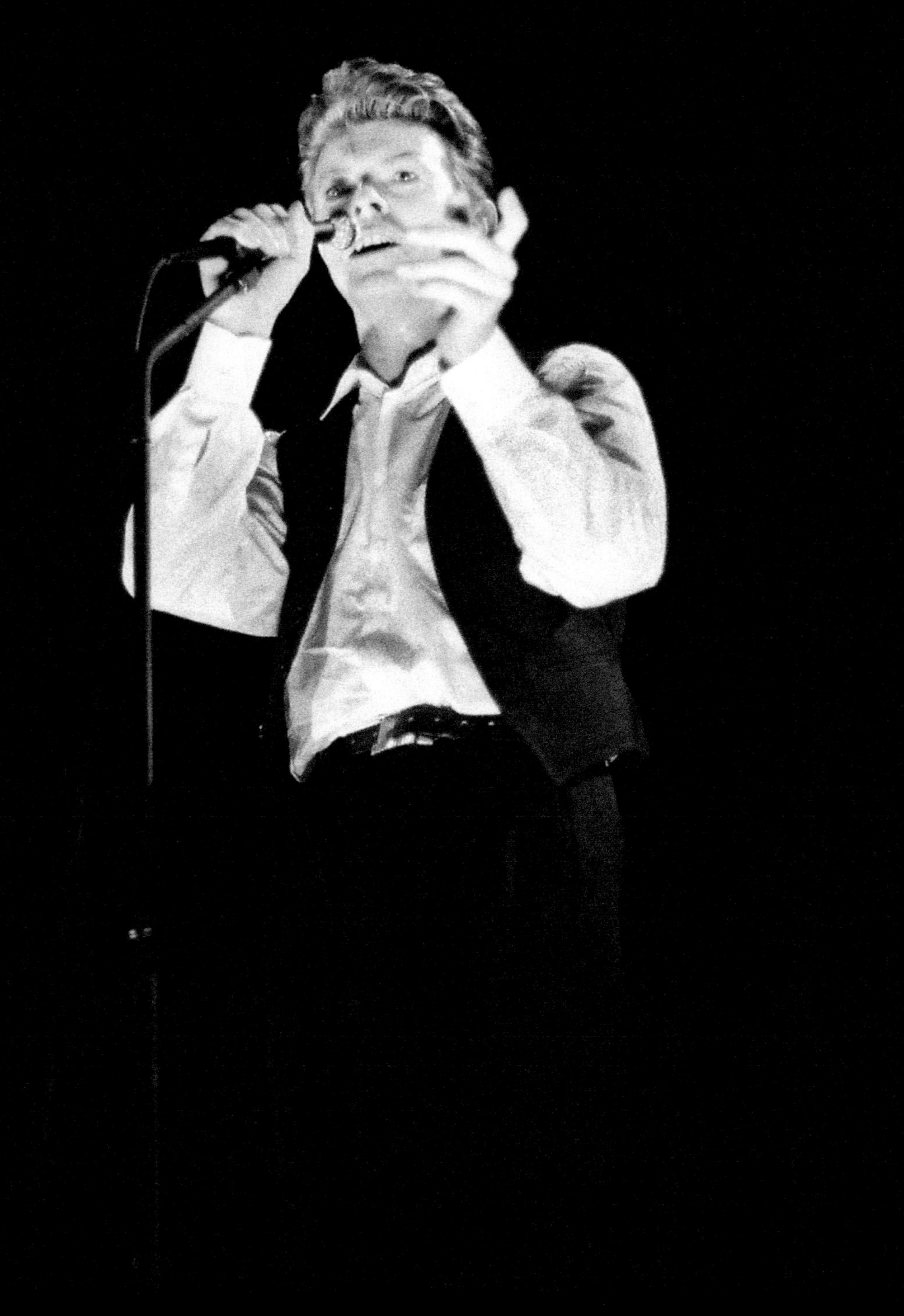

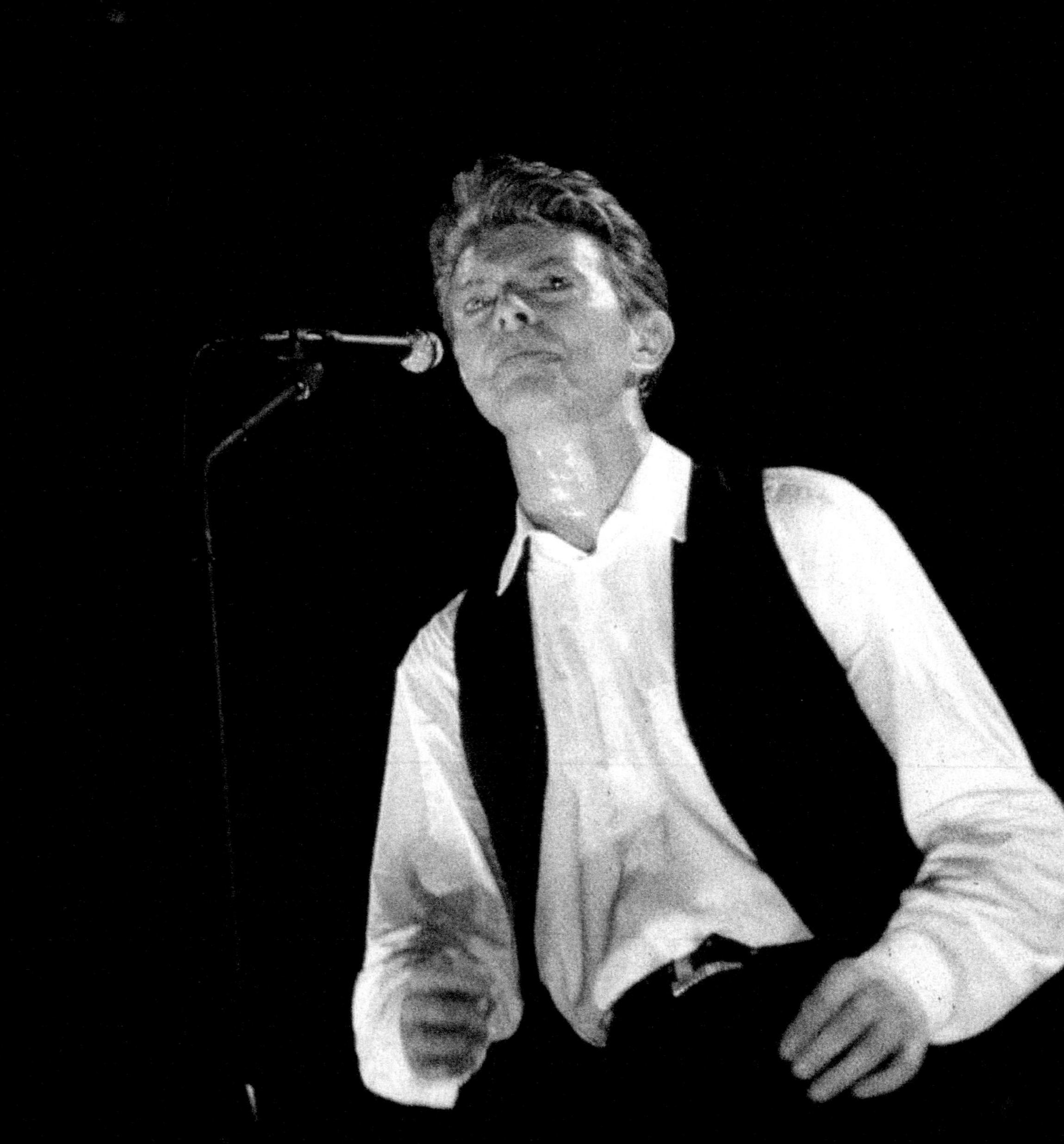

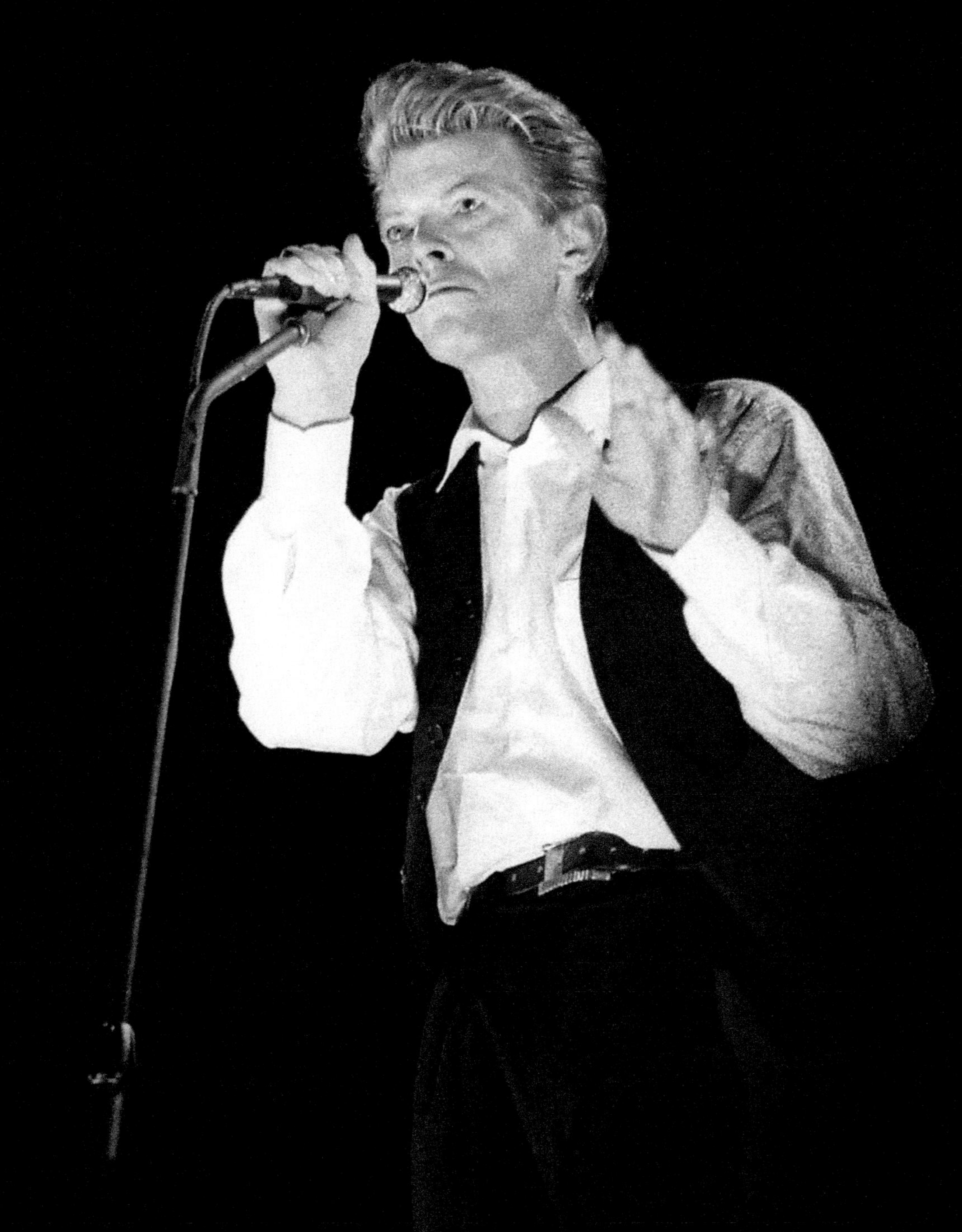

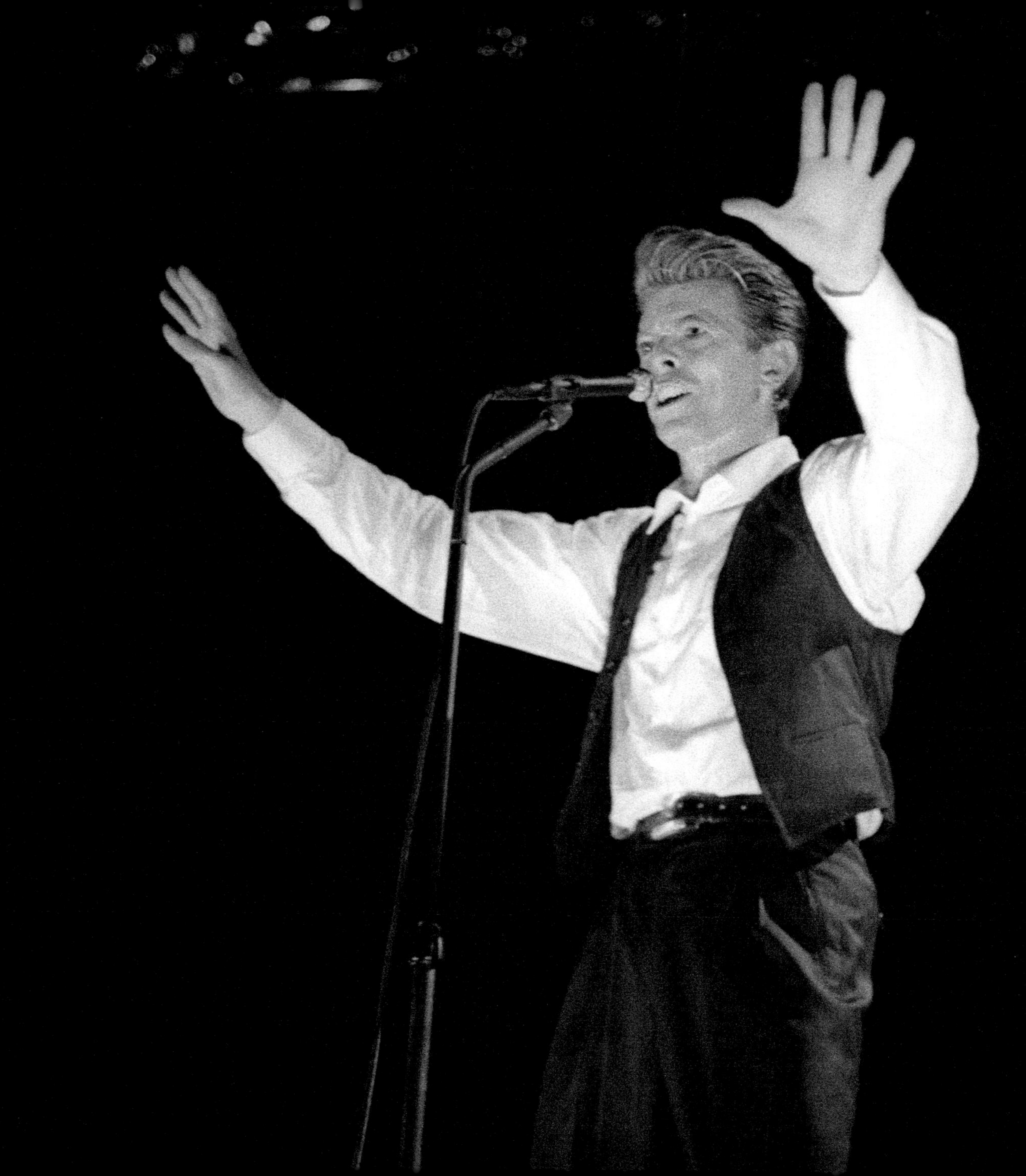

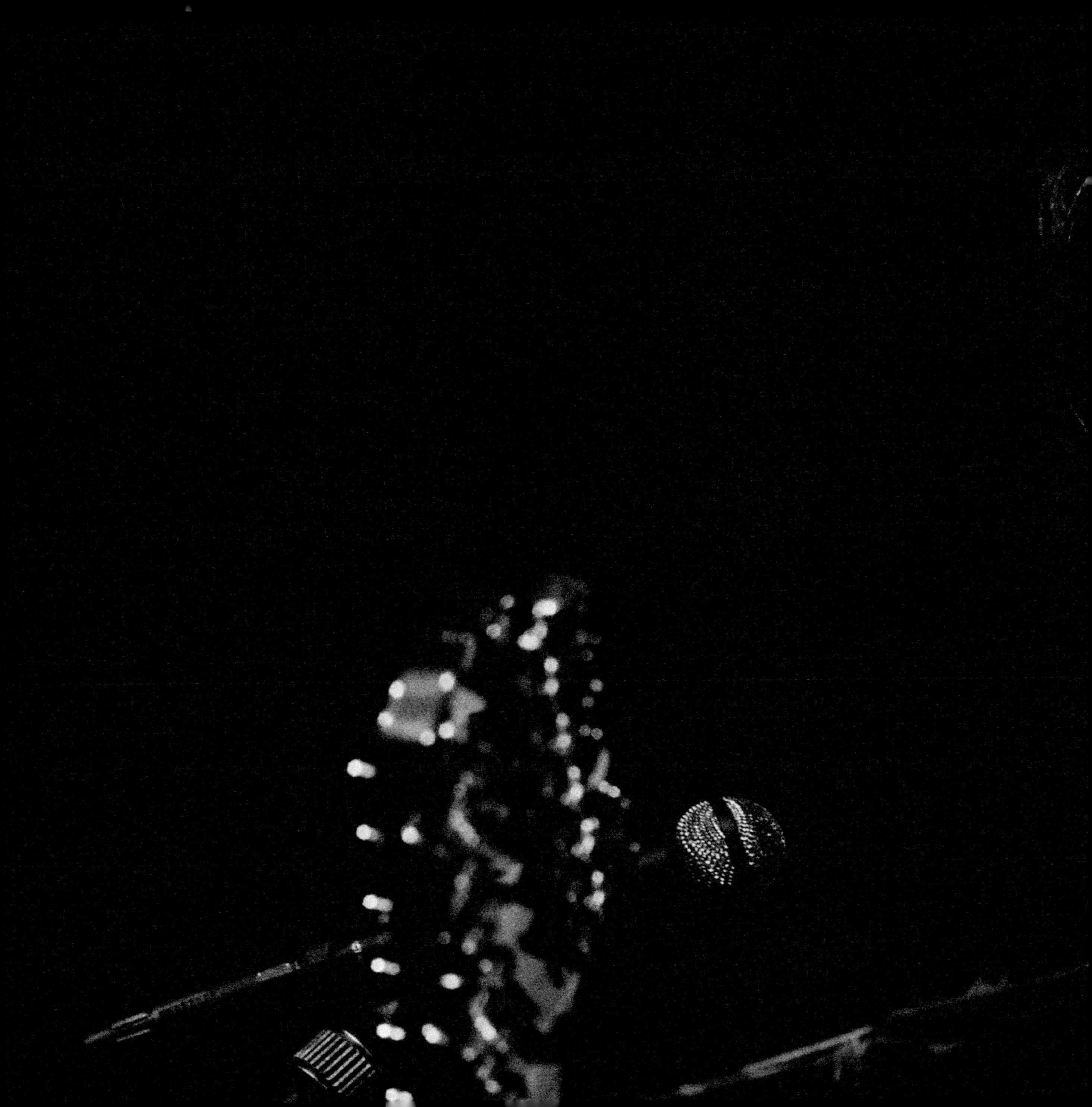

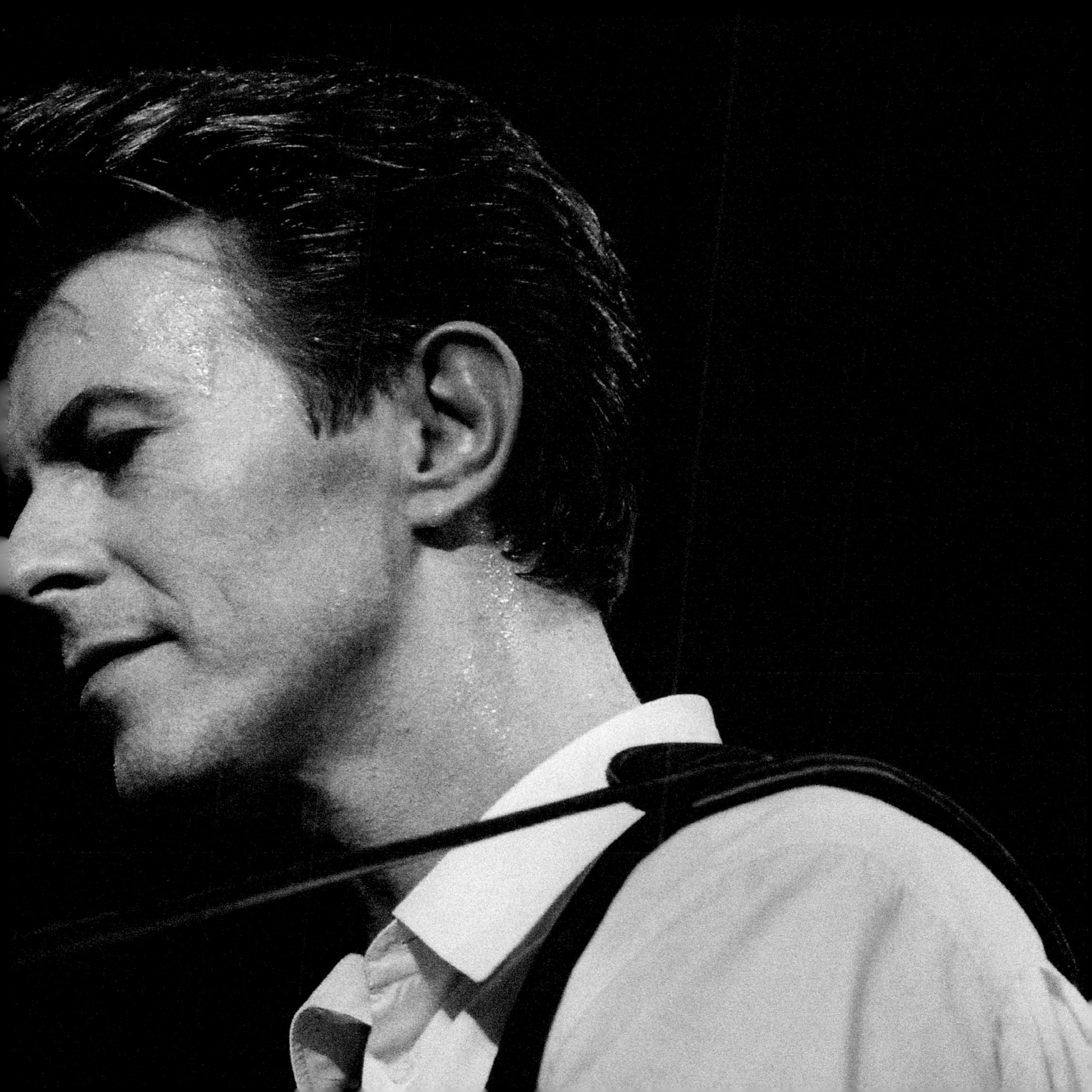

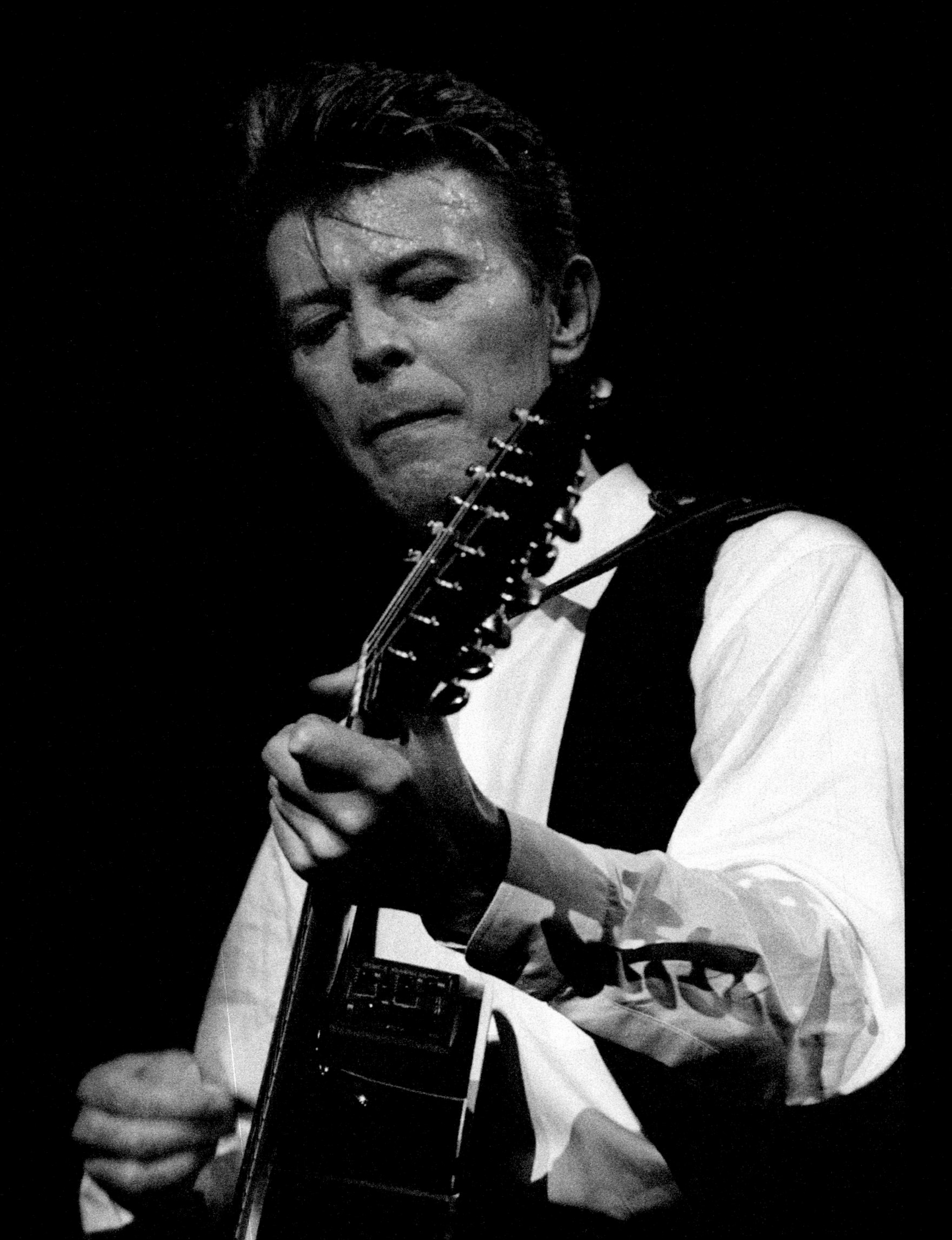

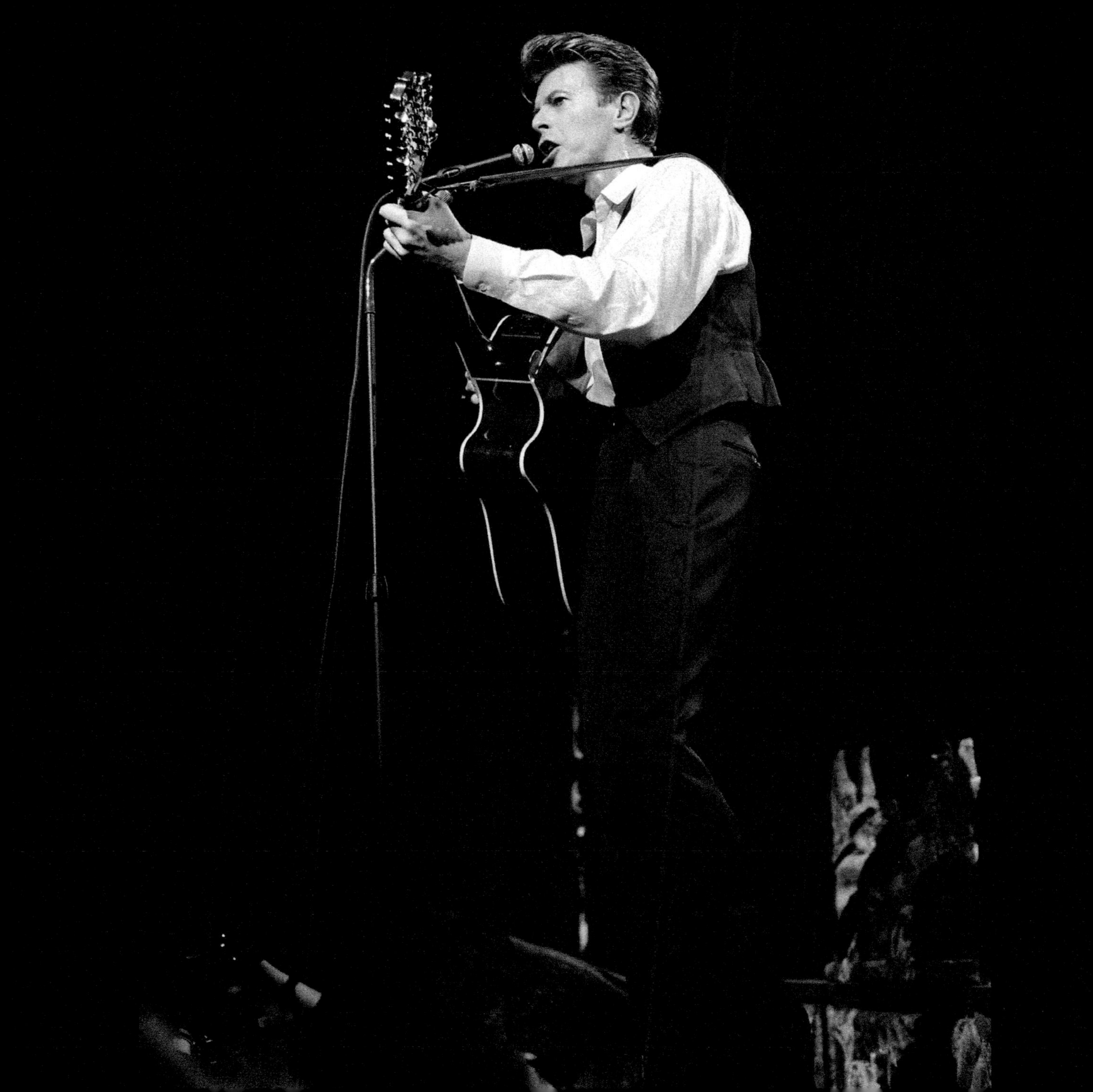

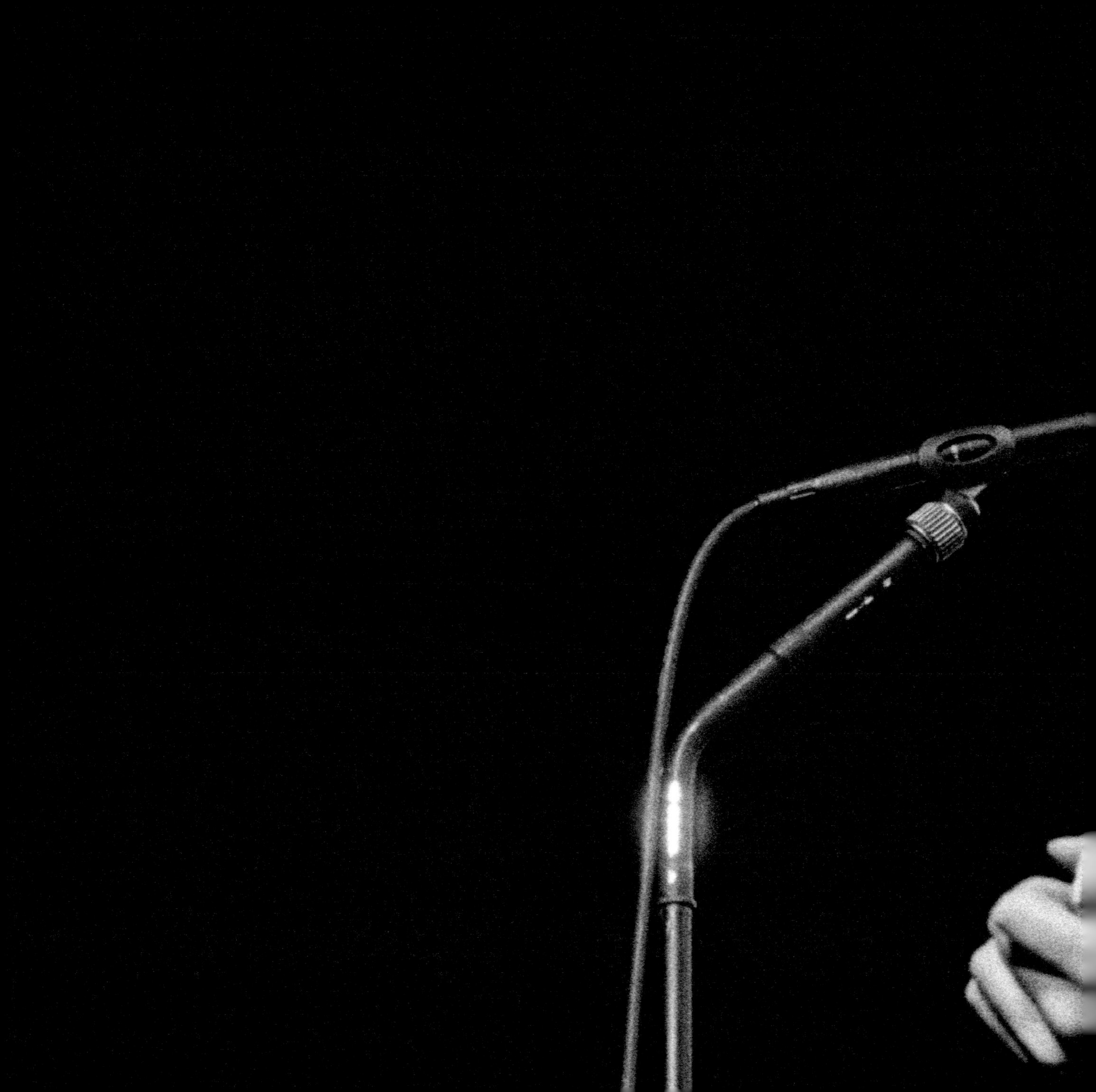

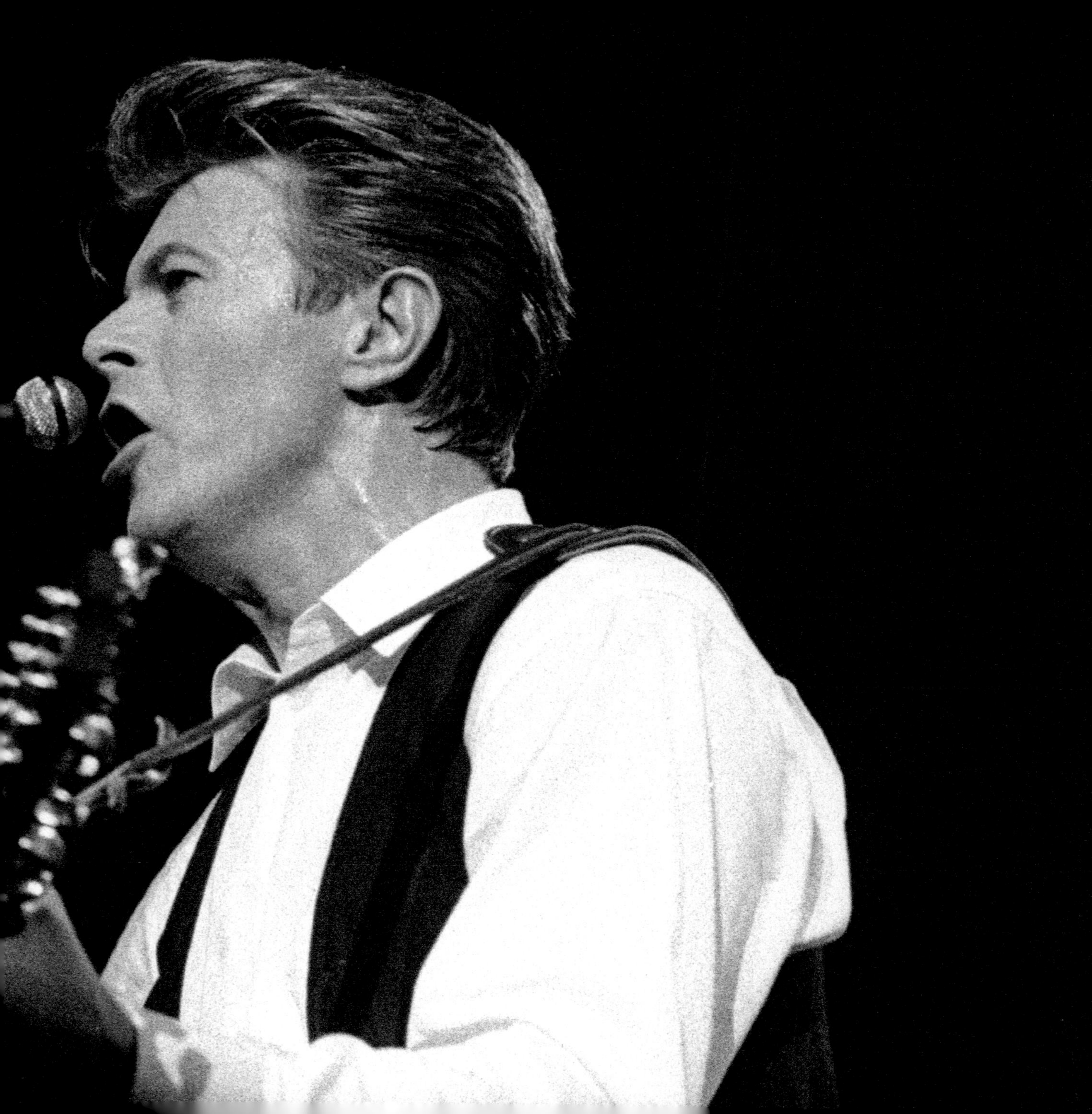

TIN MACHINE - IT'S MY LIFE TOUR

MUZIEKCENTRUM VREDENBURG UTRECHT, 28 OCTOBER 1991

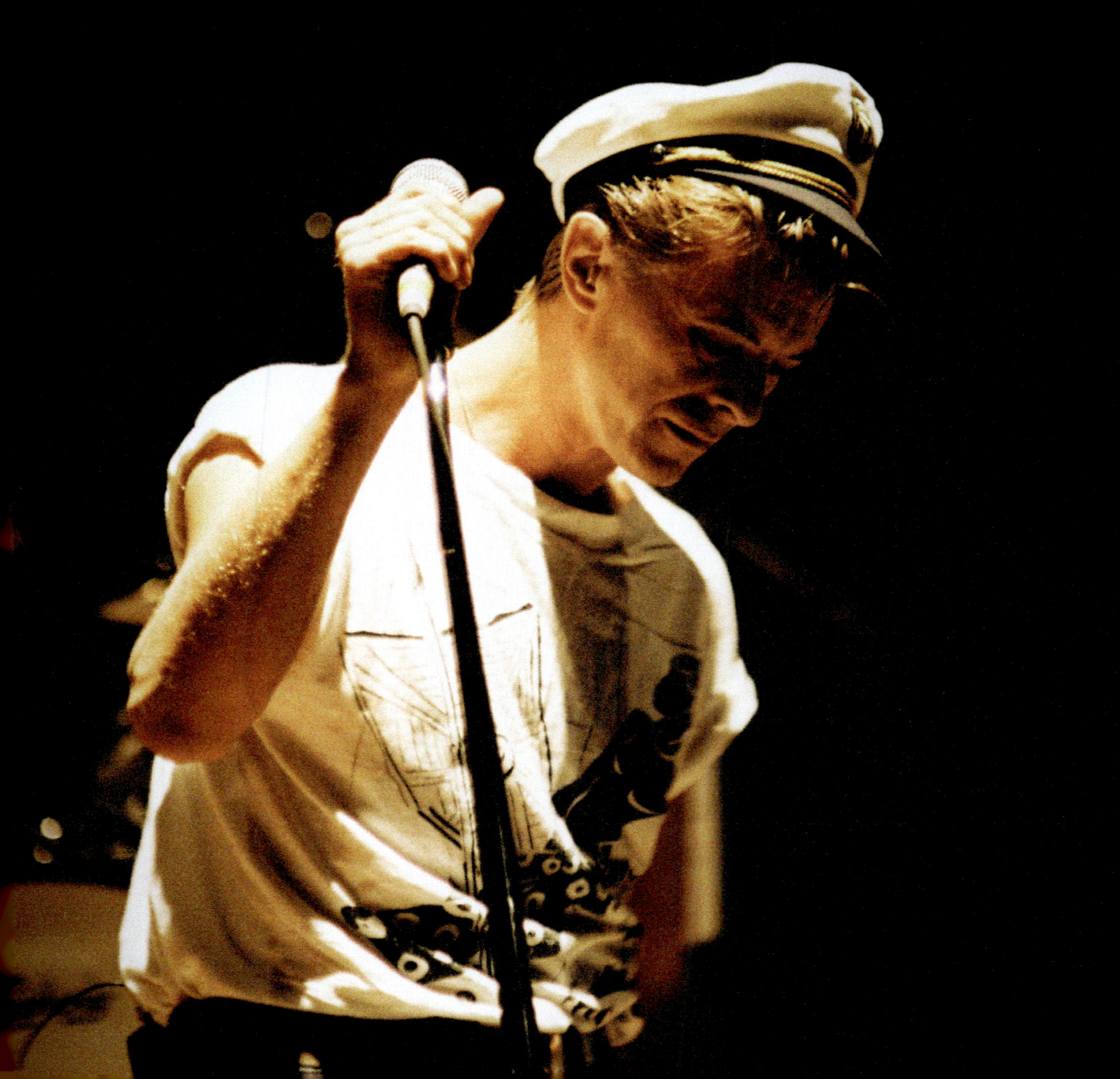

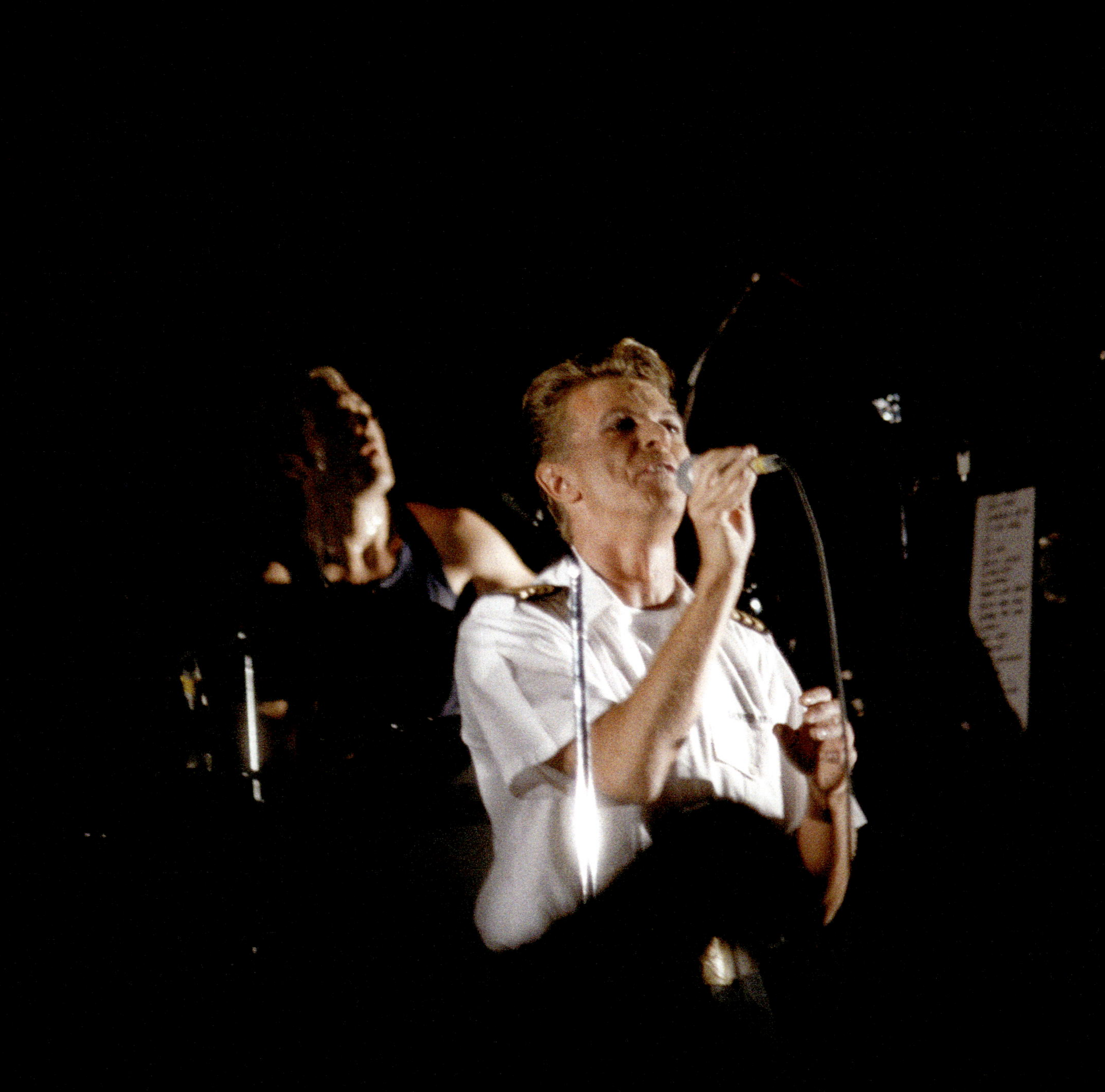

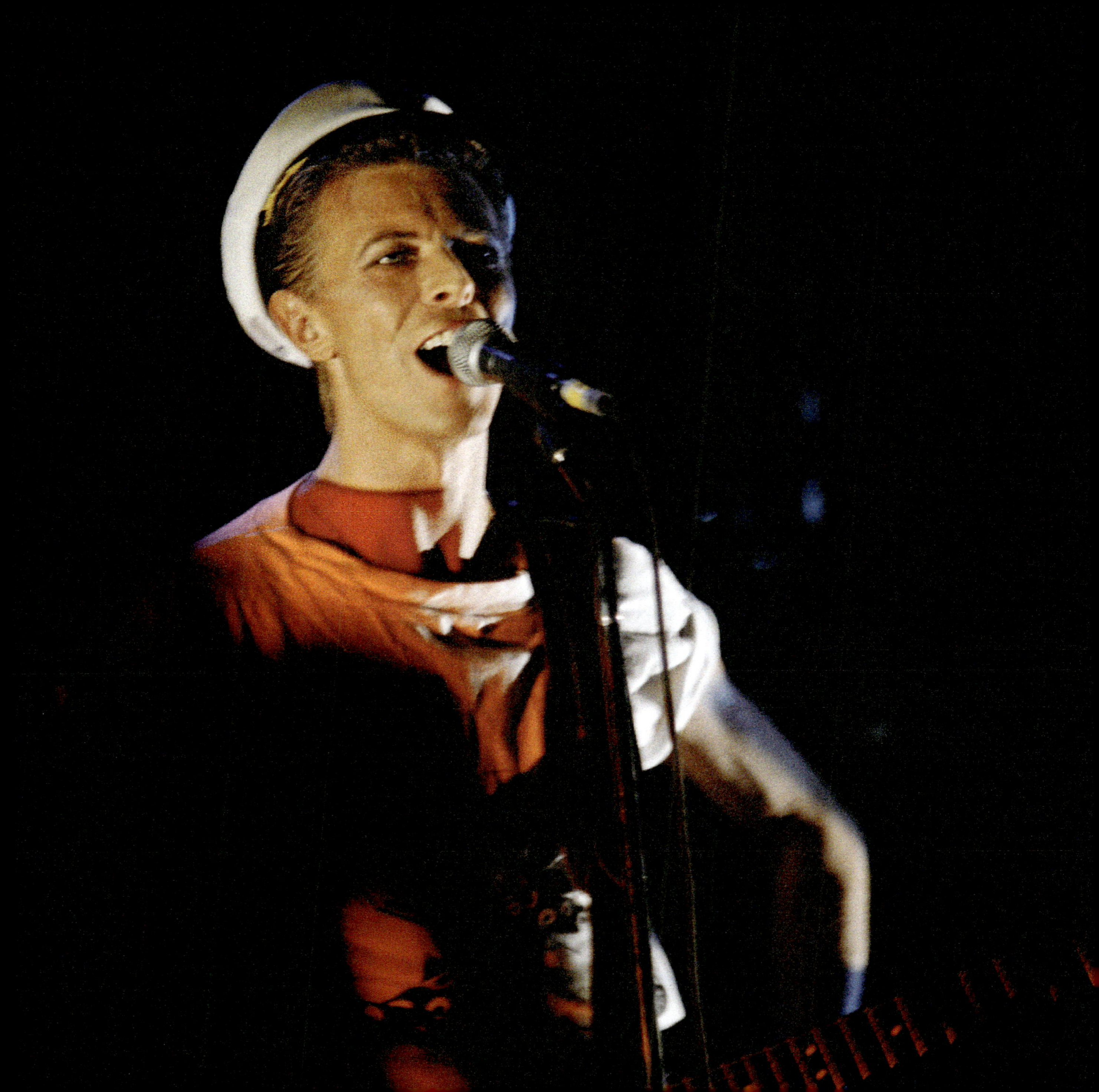

OUTSIDE TOUR

PRINS VAN ORANJEHAL UTRECHT, 28 JANUARY 1996

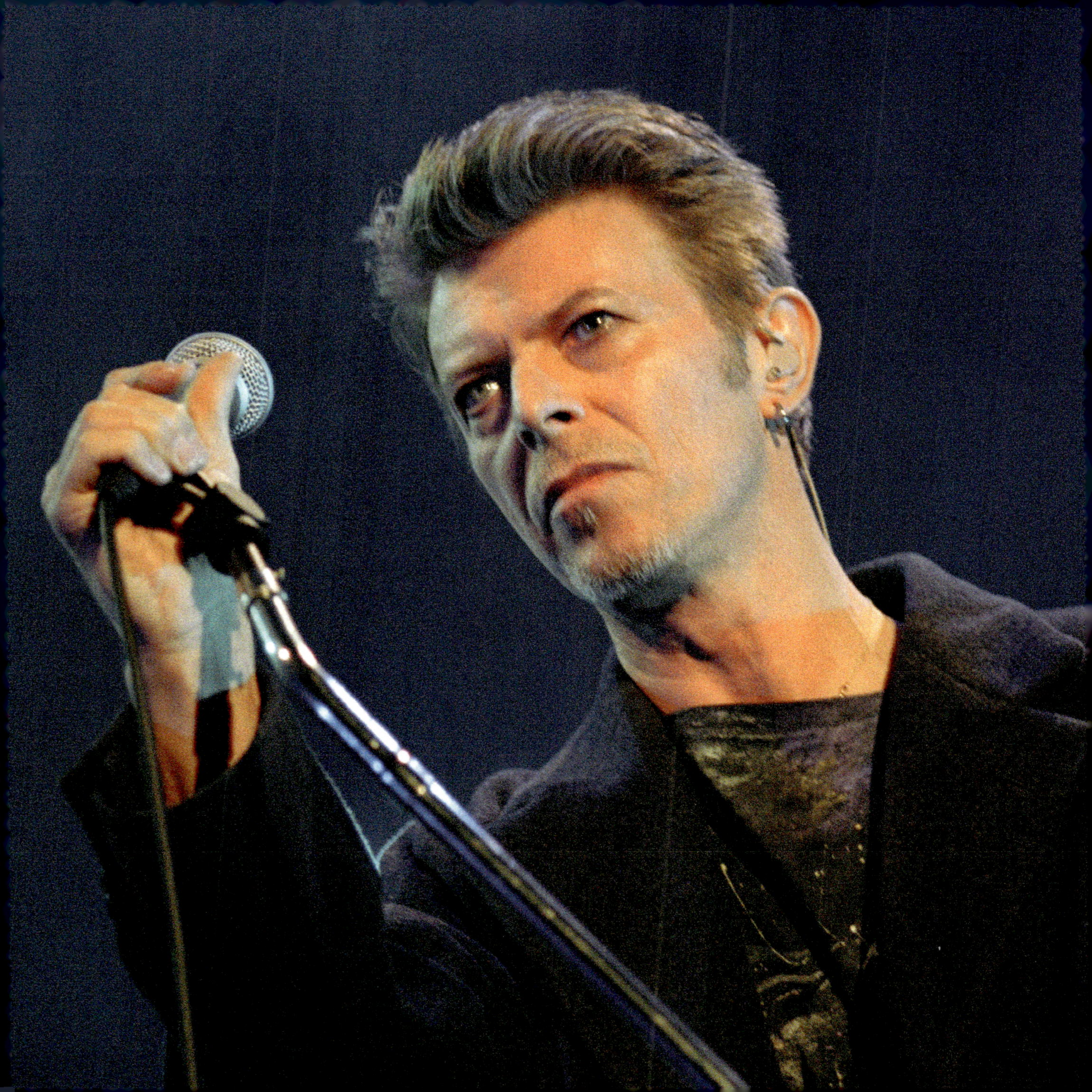

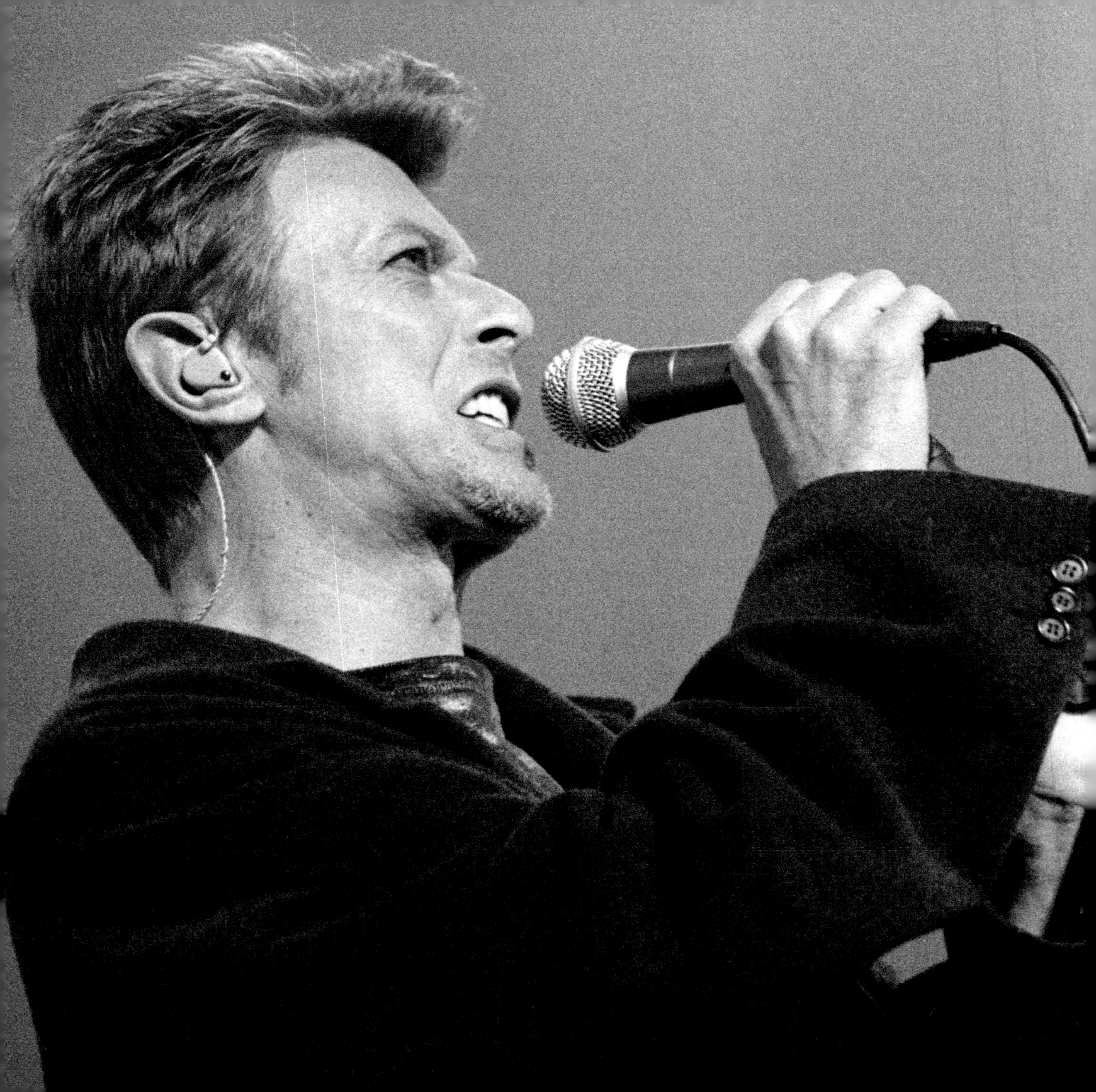

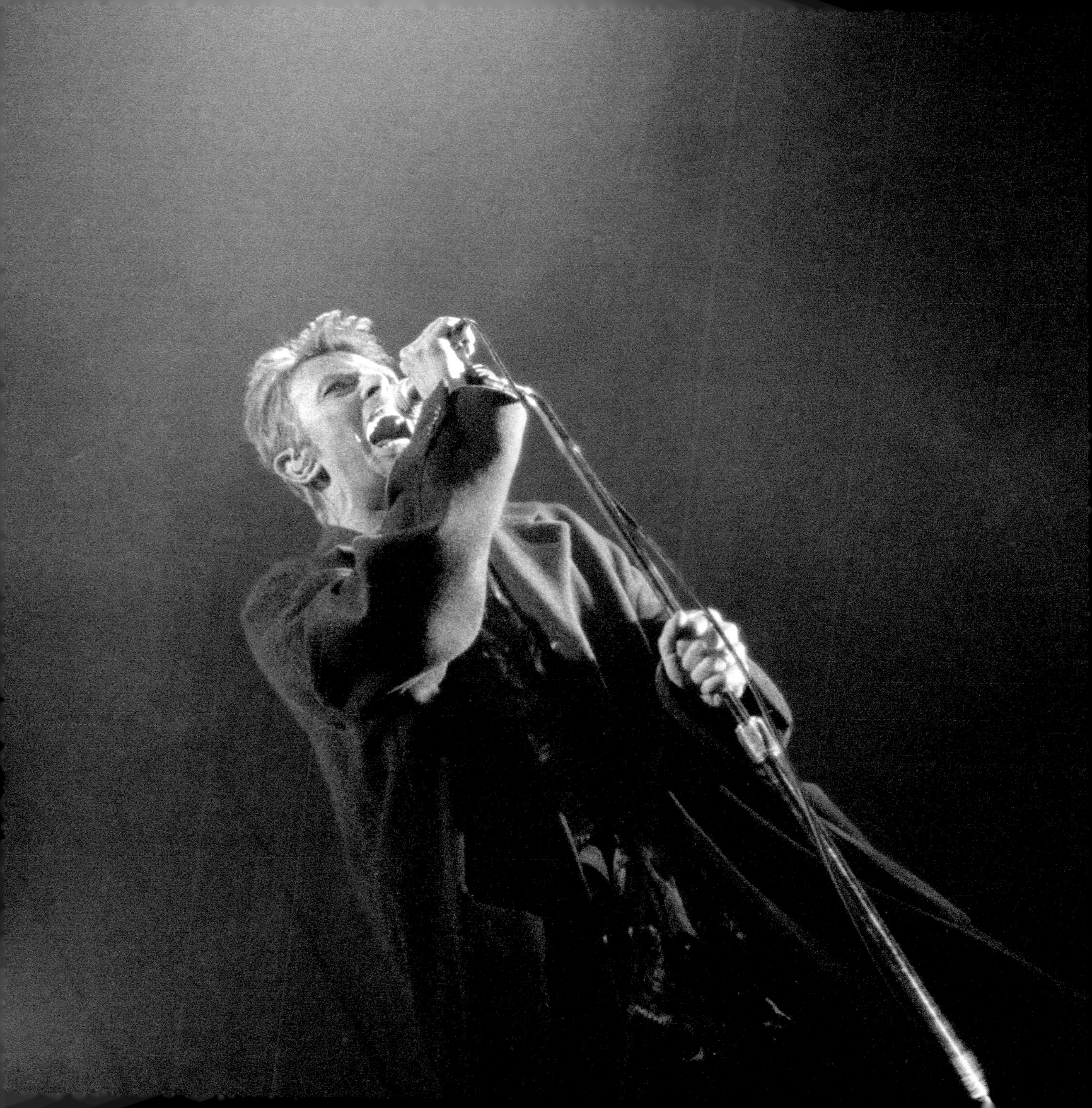

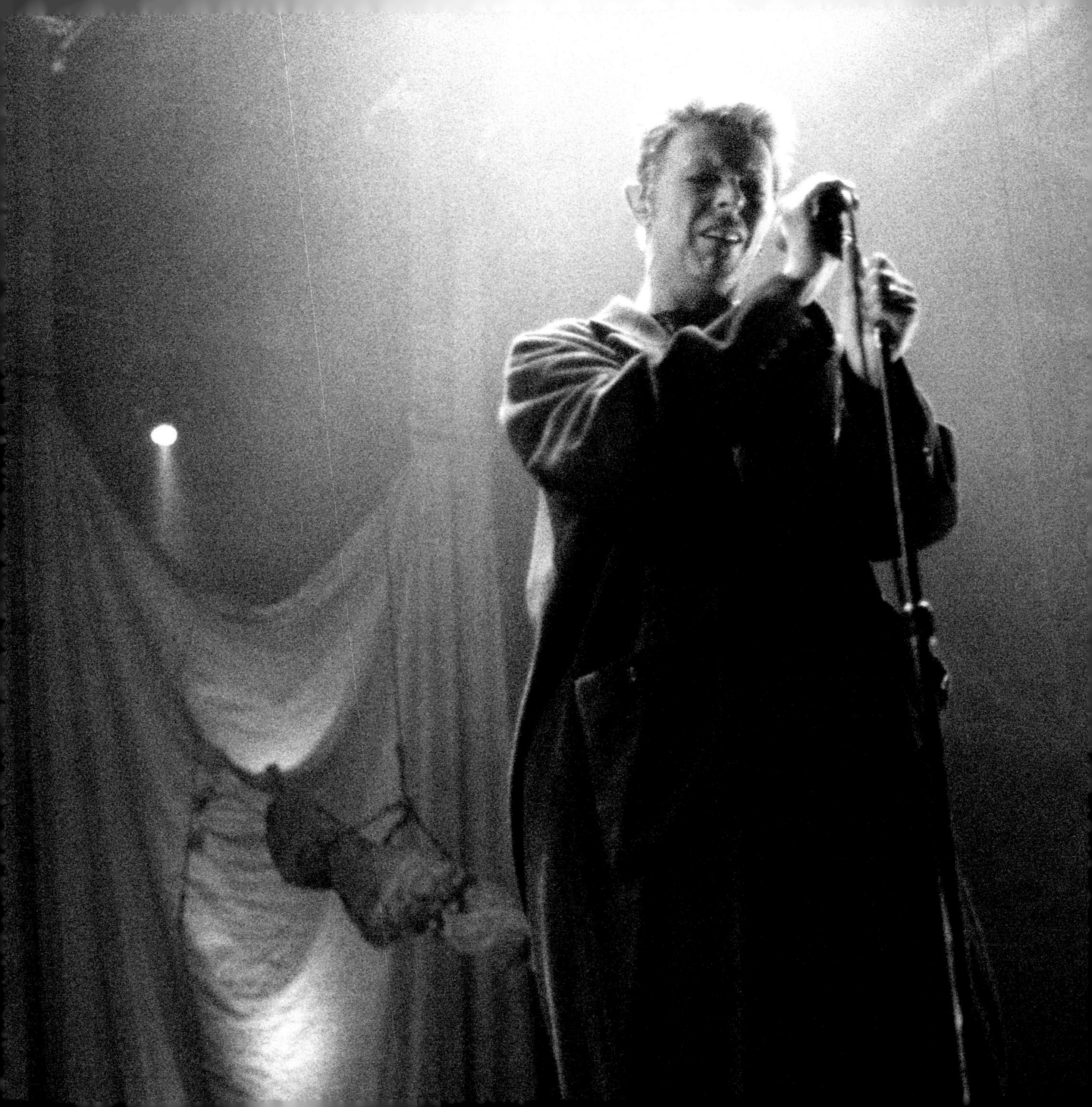

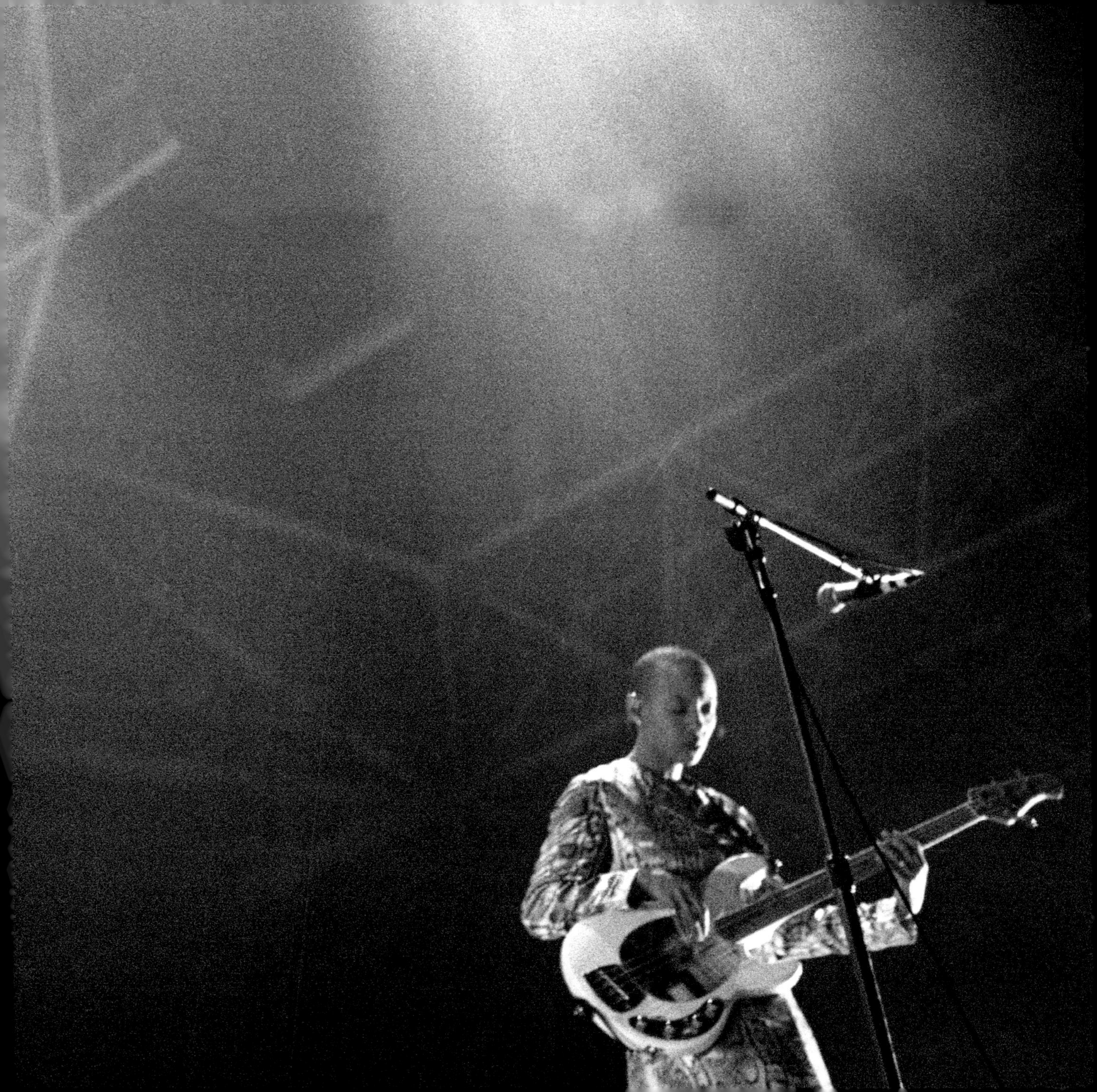

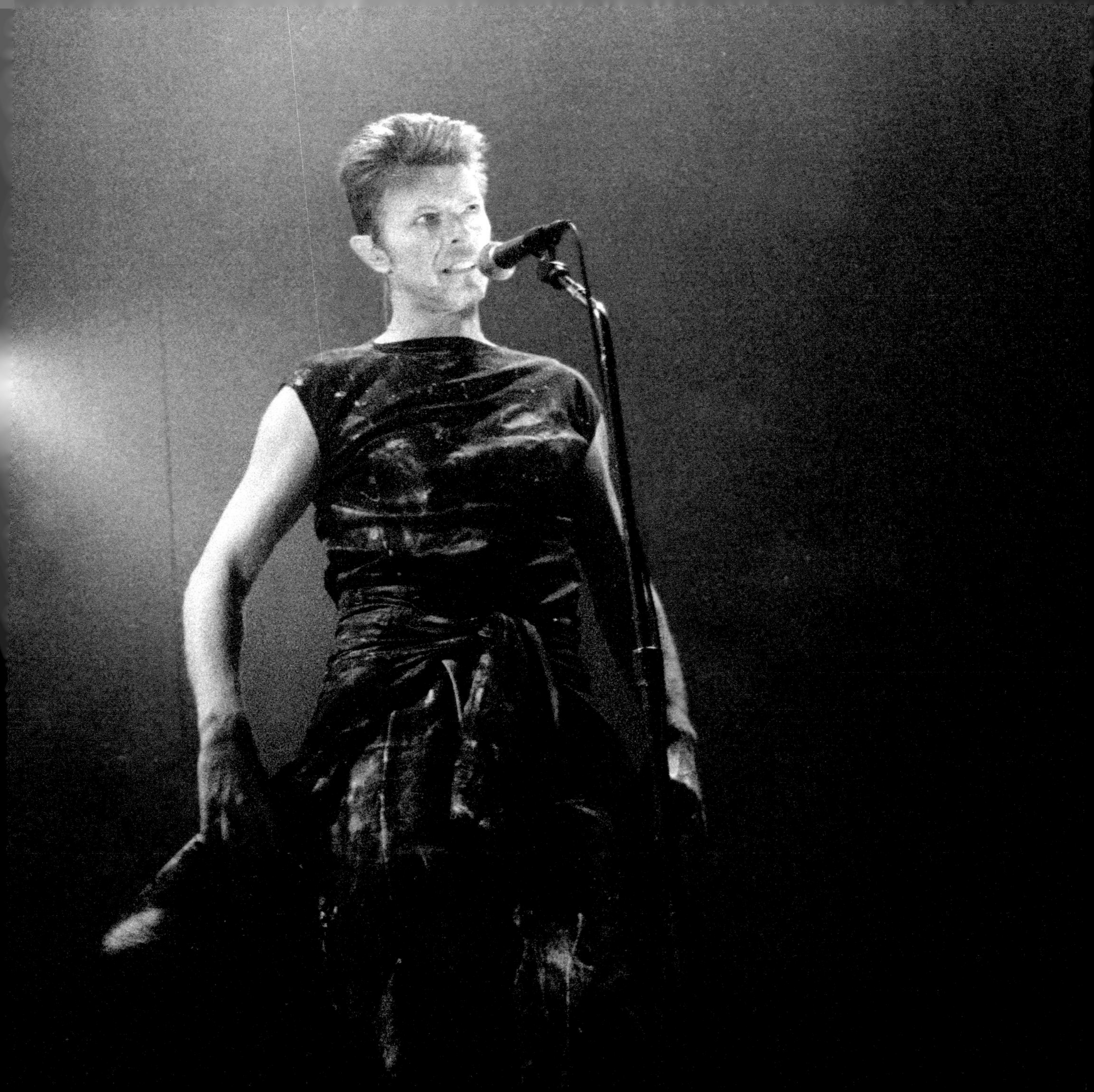

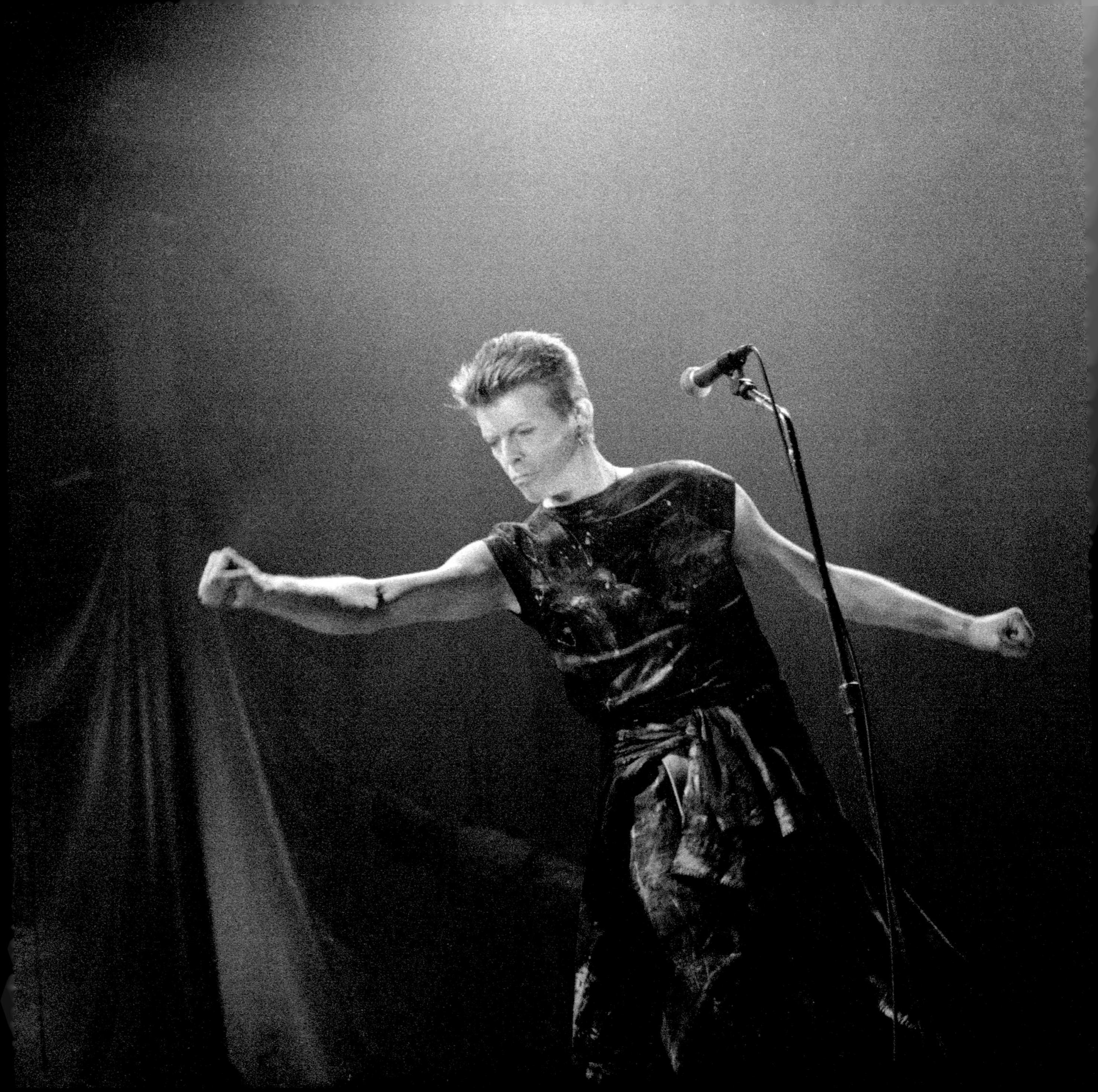

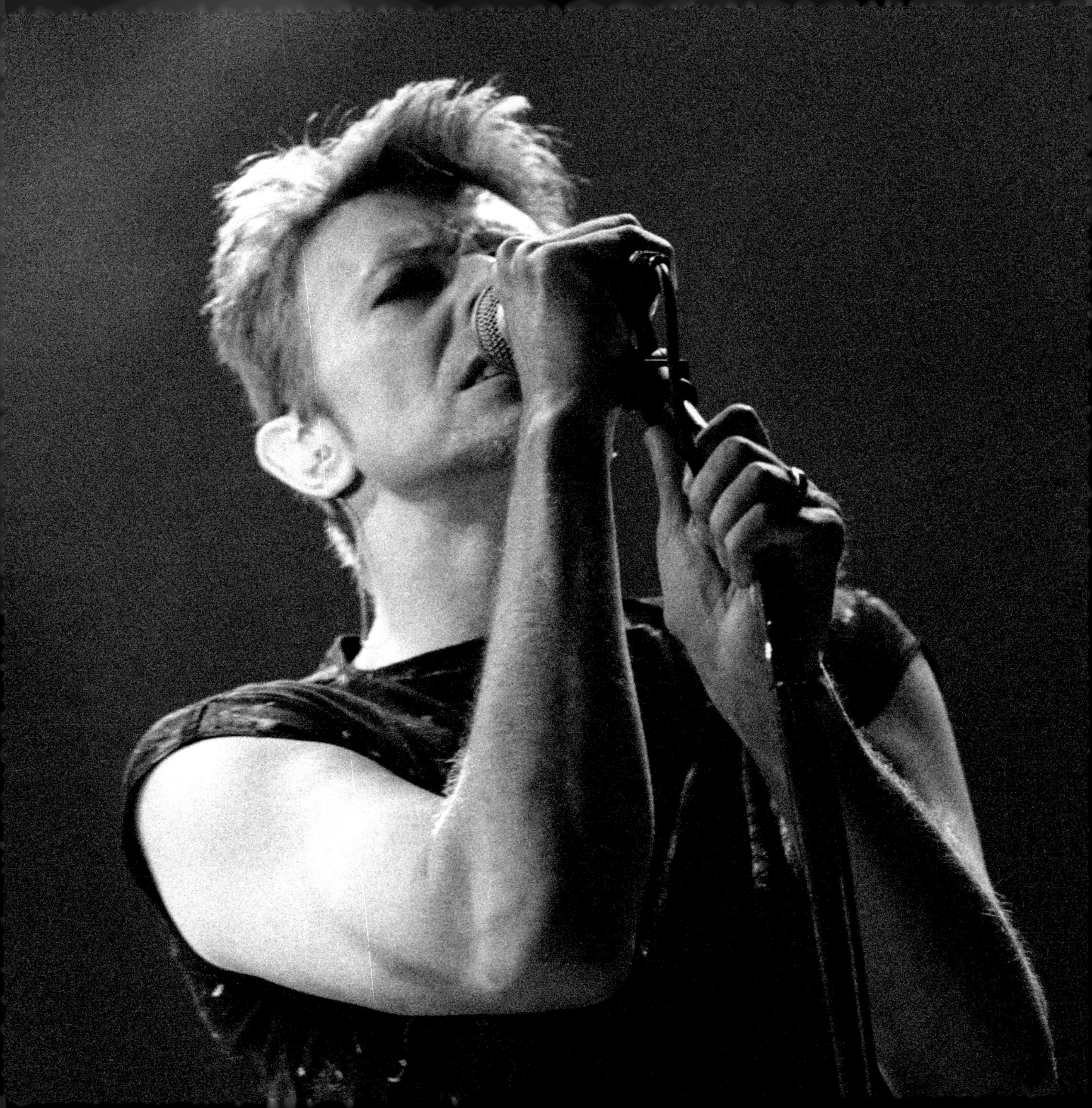

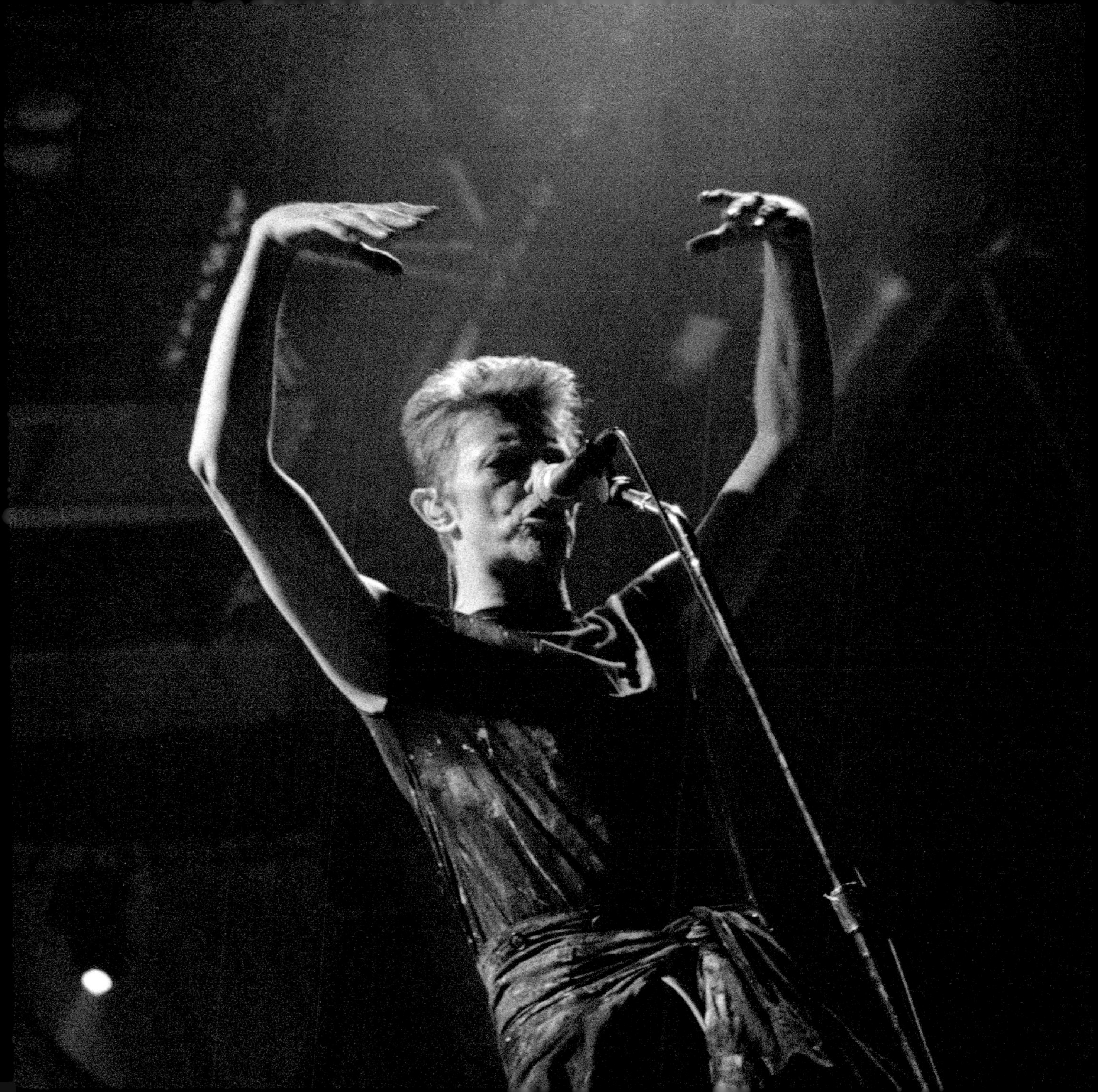

OUTSIDE SUMMER FESTIVALS TOUR

SPORTPALEIS AHOY ROTTERDAM, 16 JULY 1996

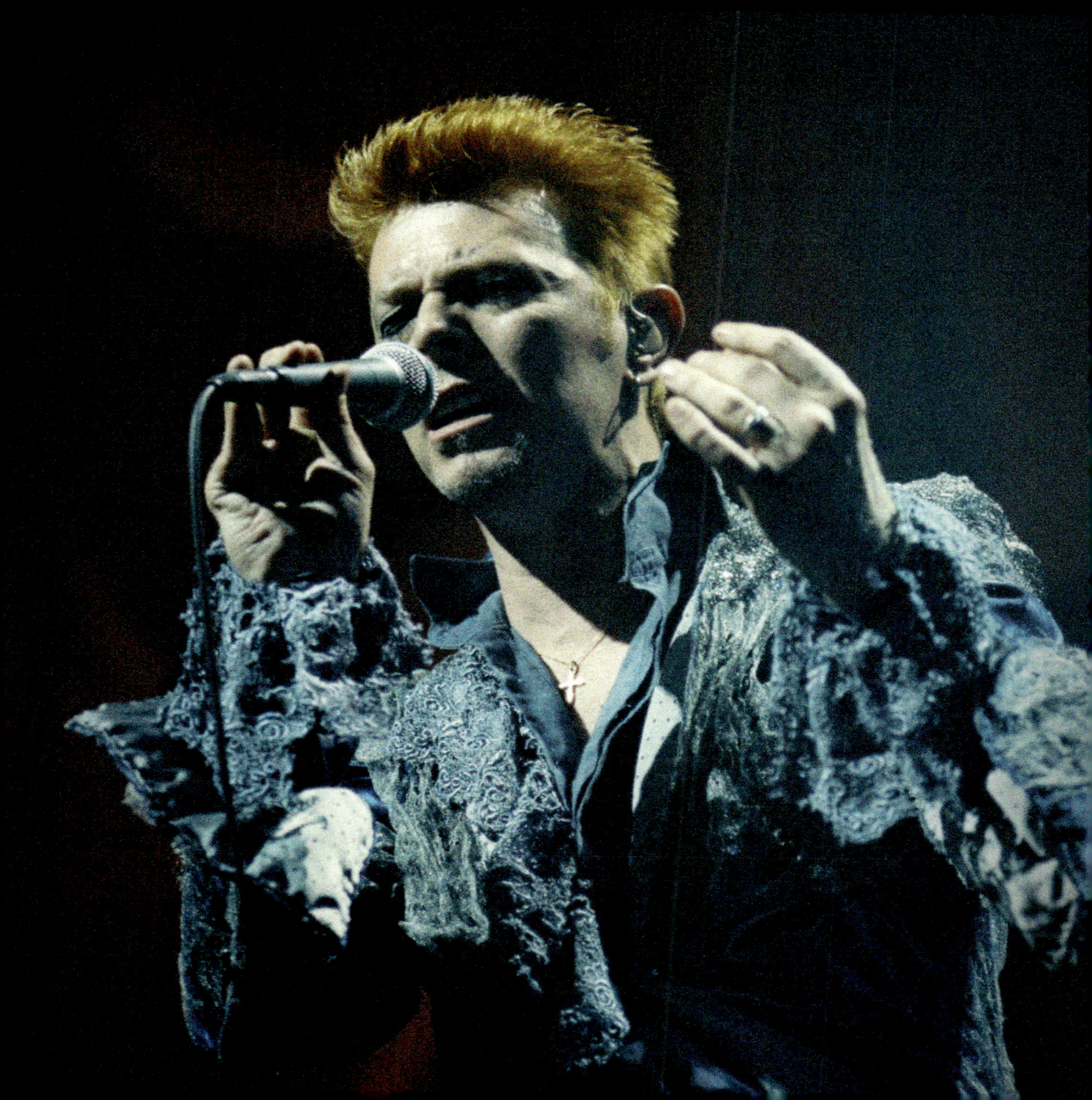

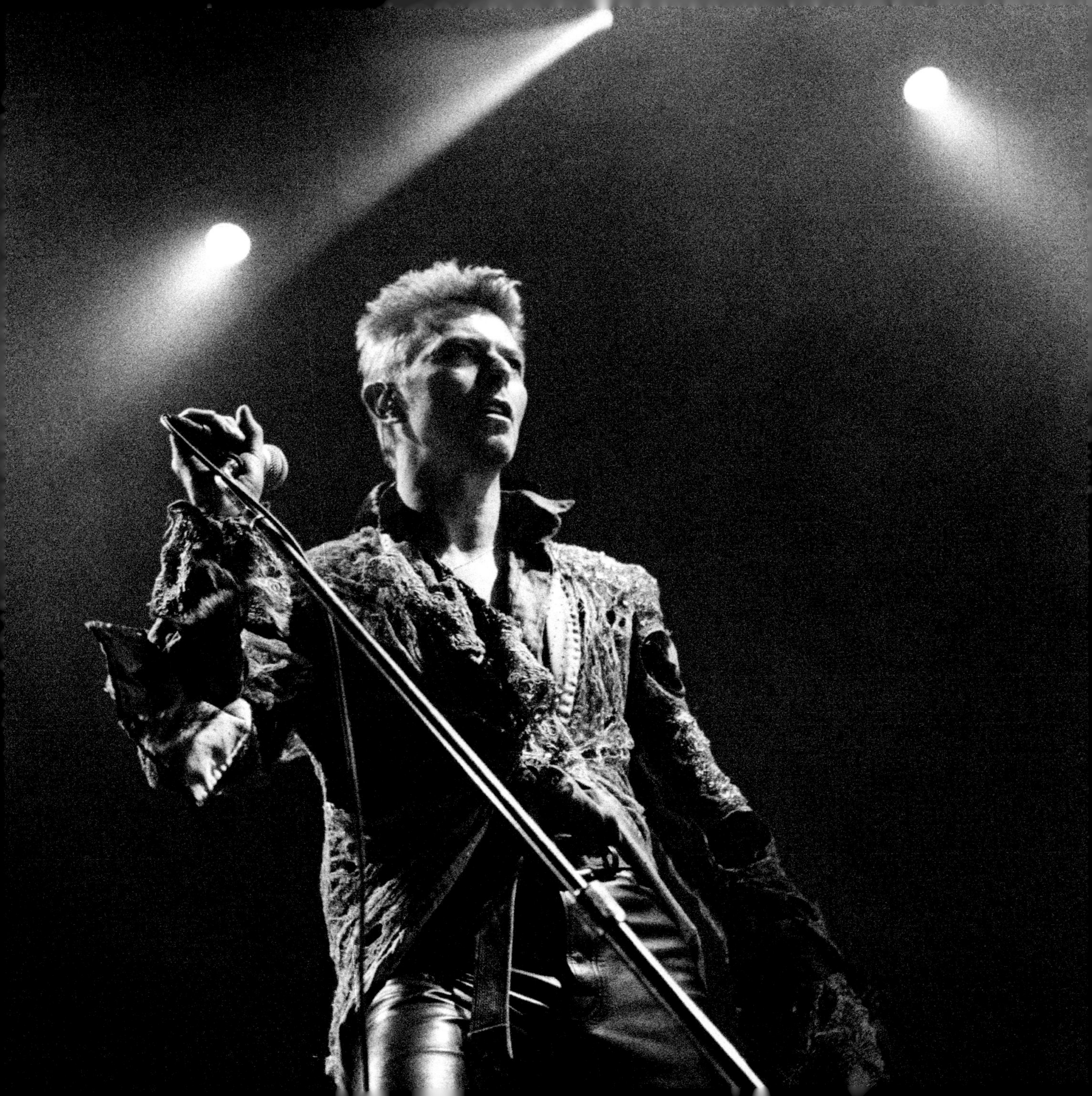

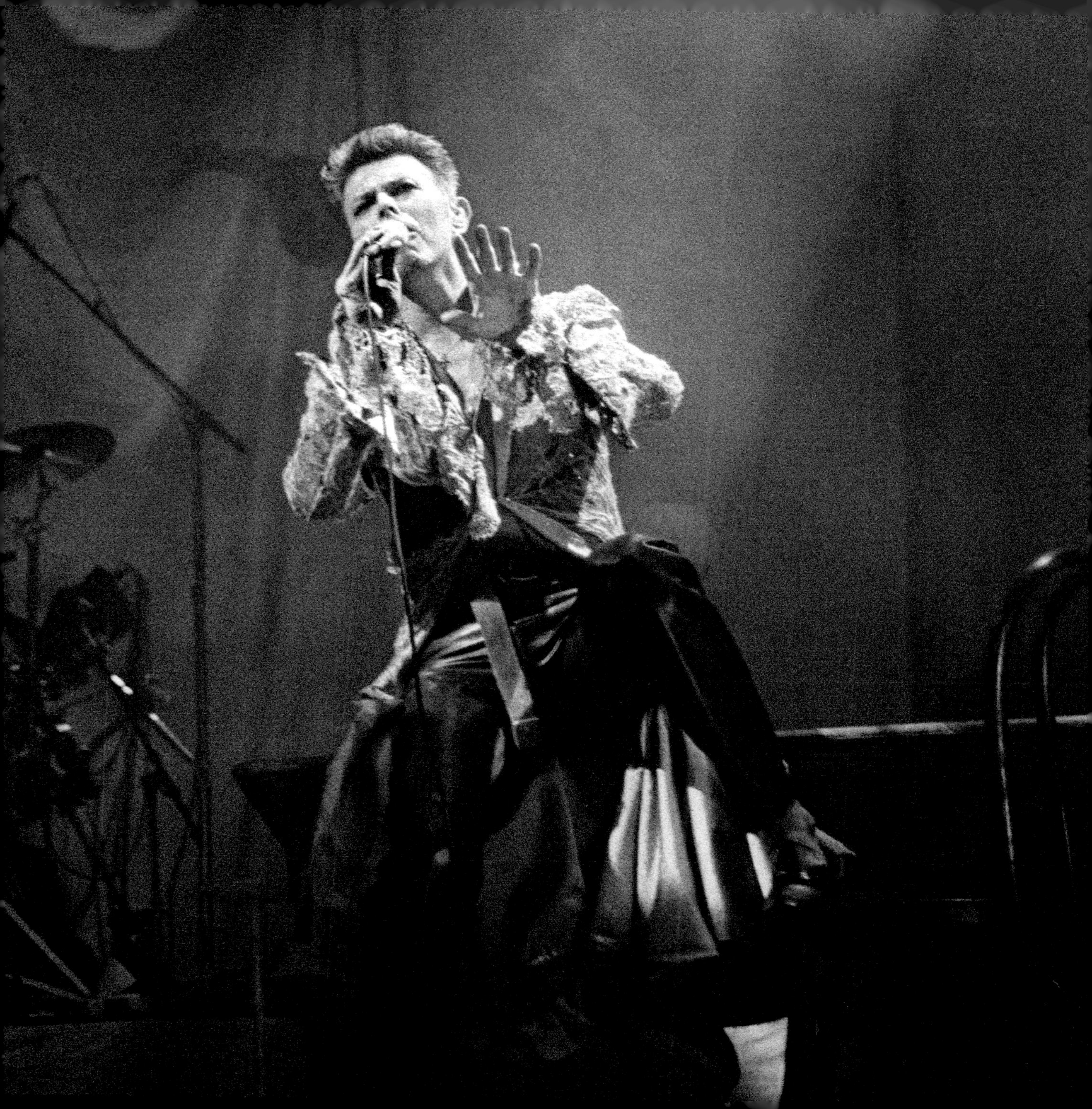

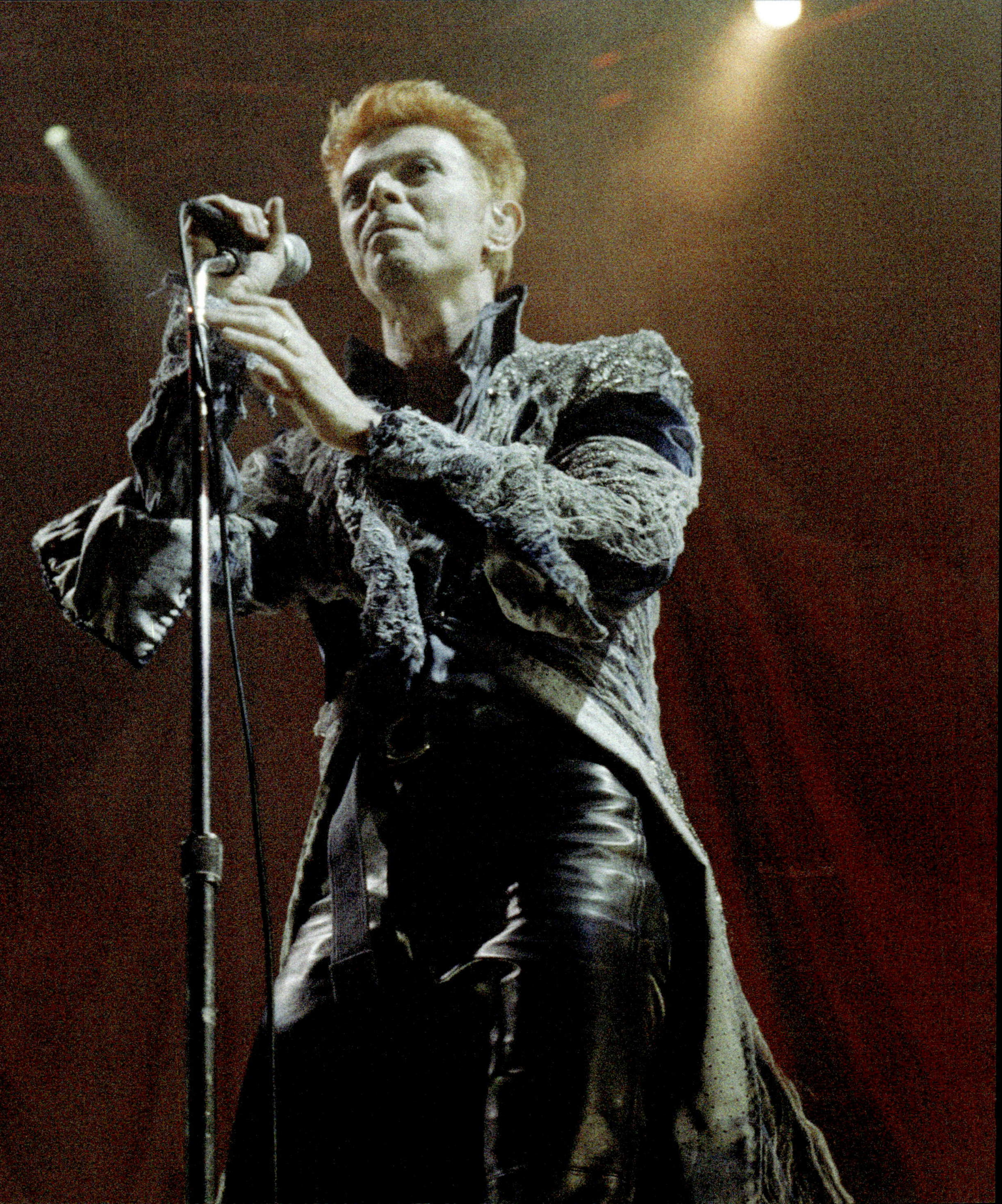

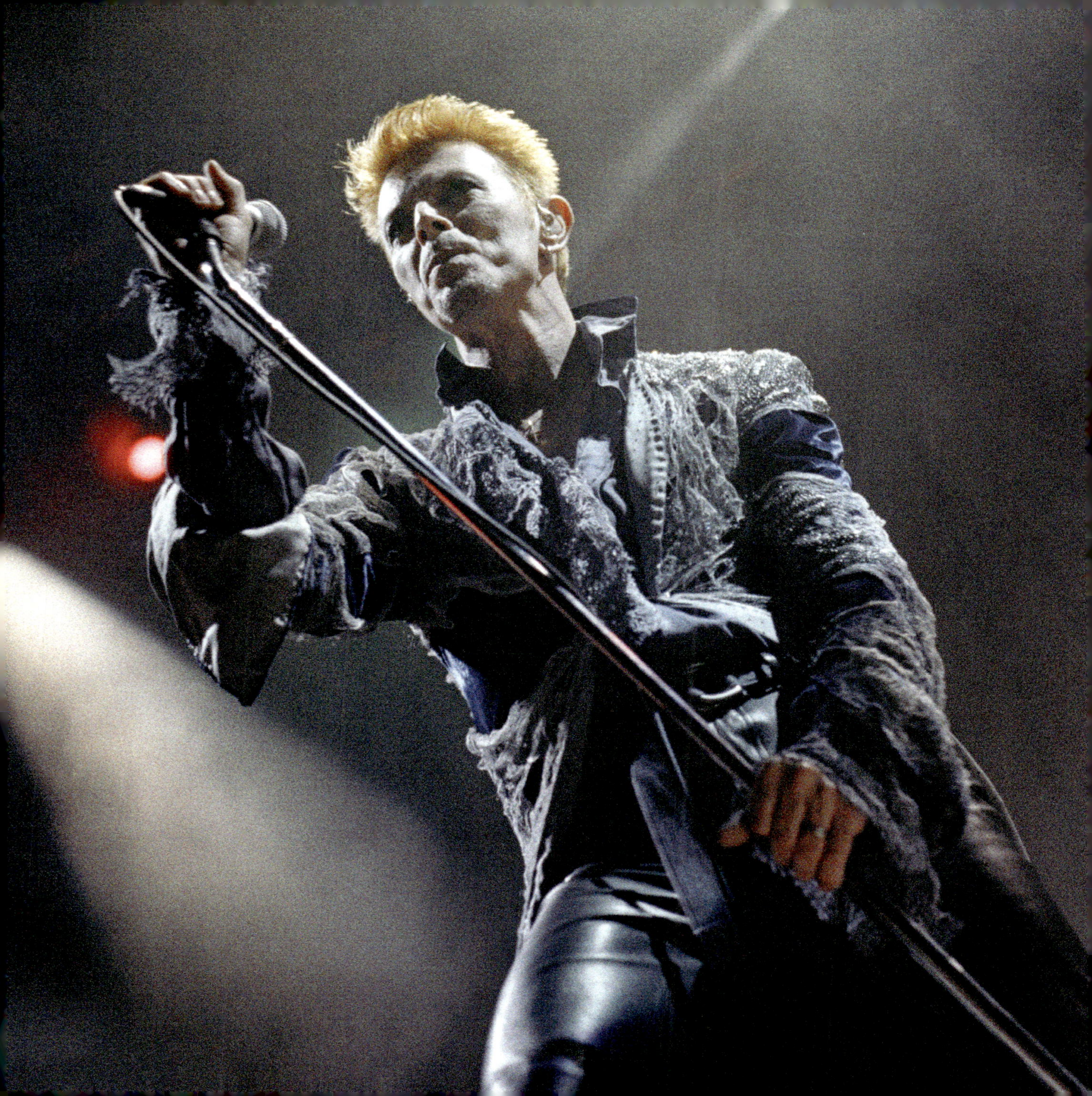

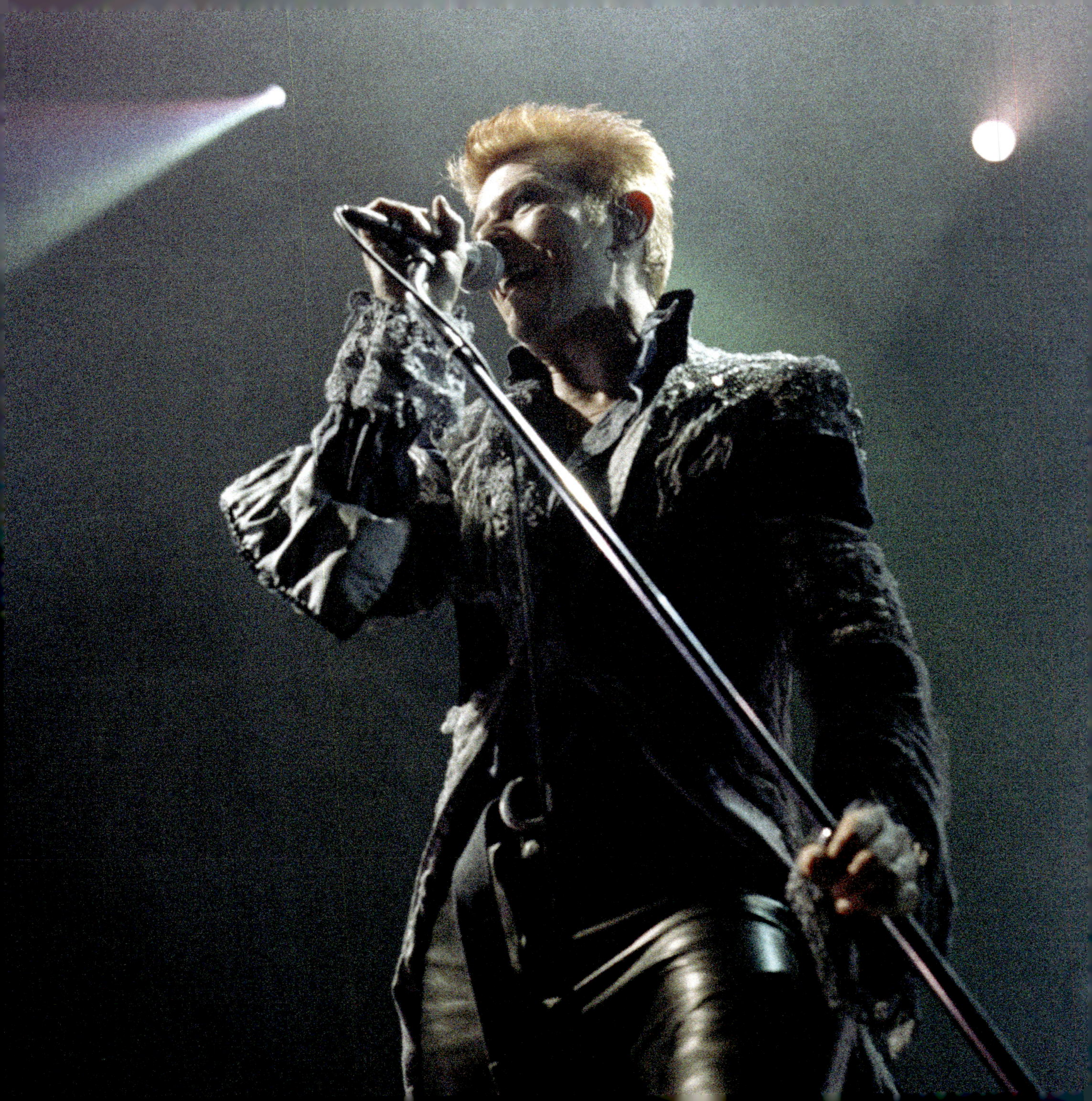

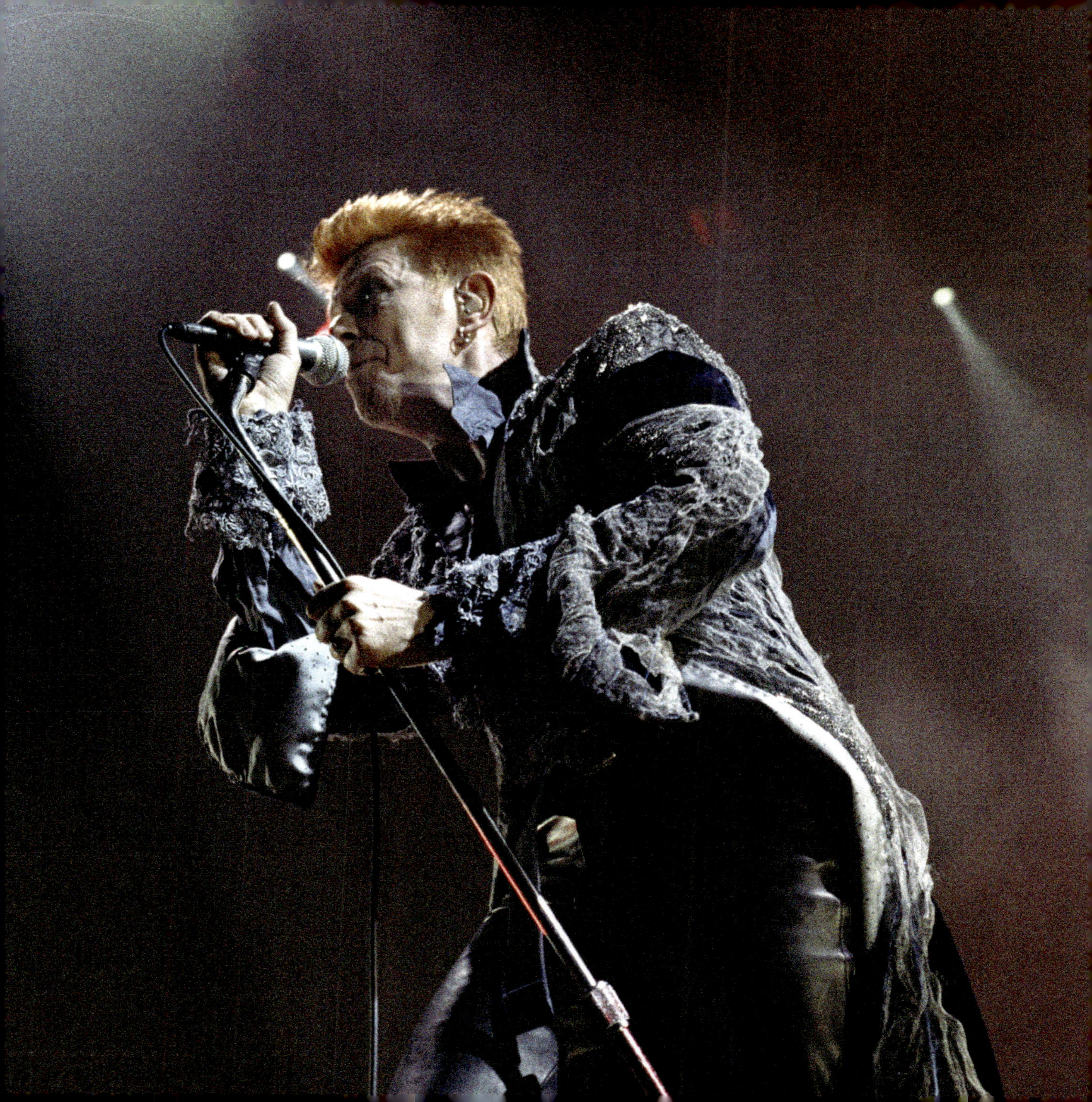

EARTHLING TOUR

MUZIEKCENTRUM VREDENBURG UTRECHT, 16 JUNE 1997

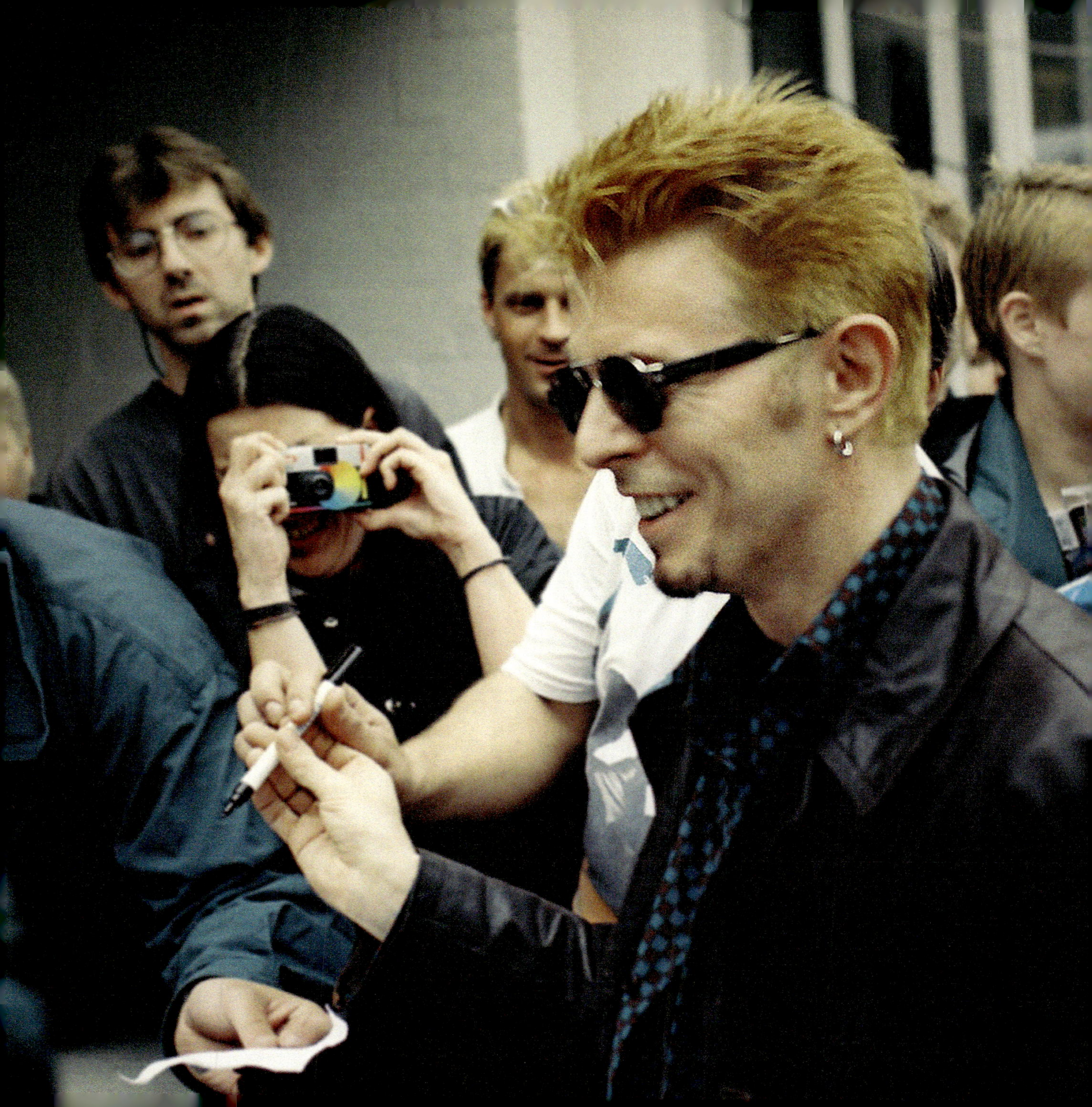

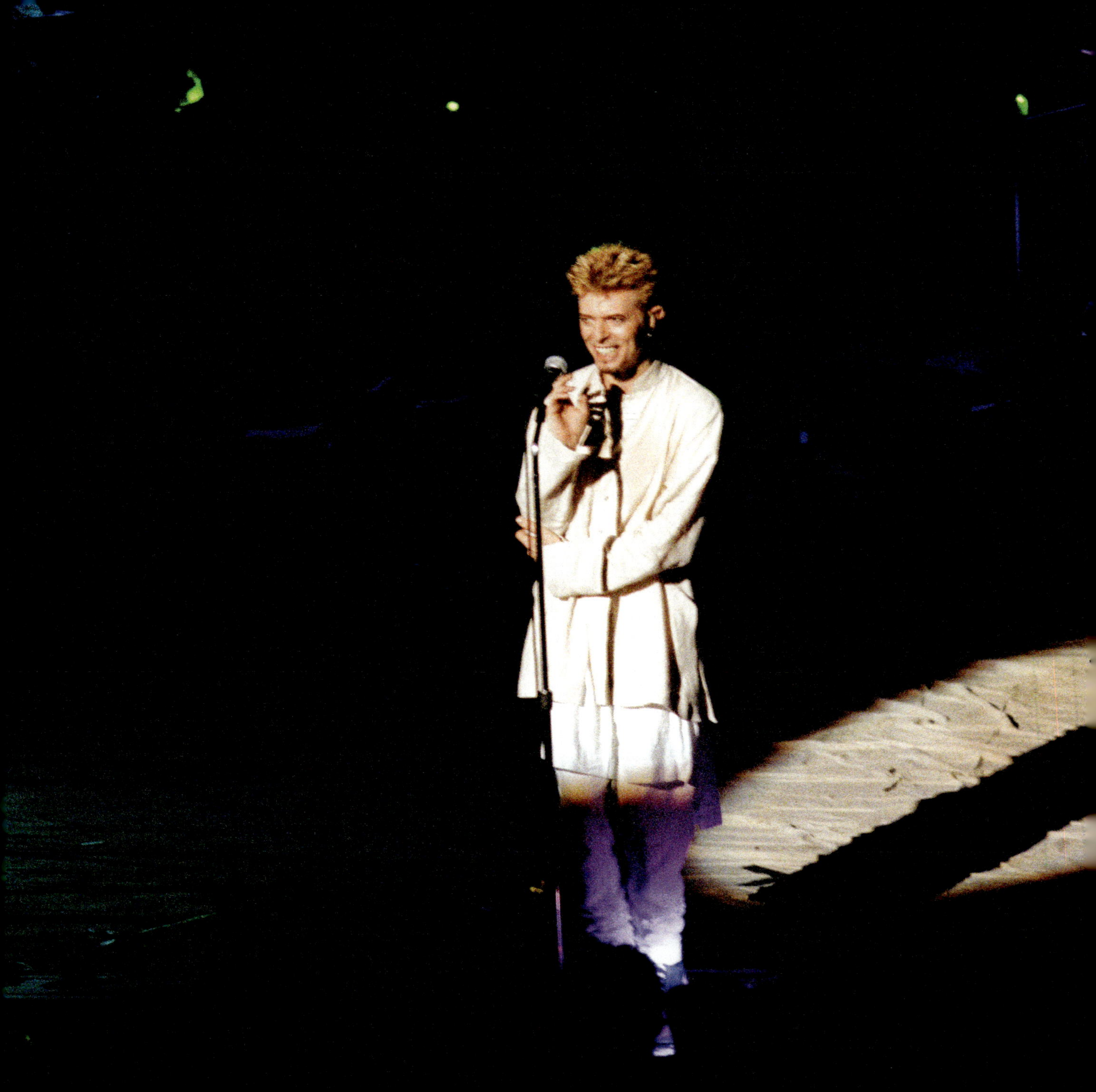

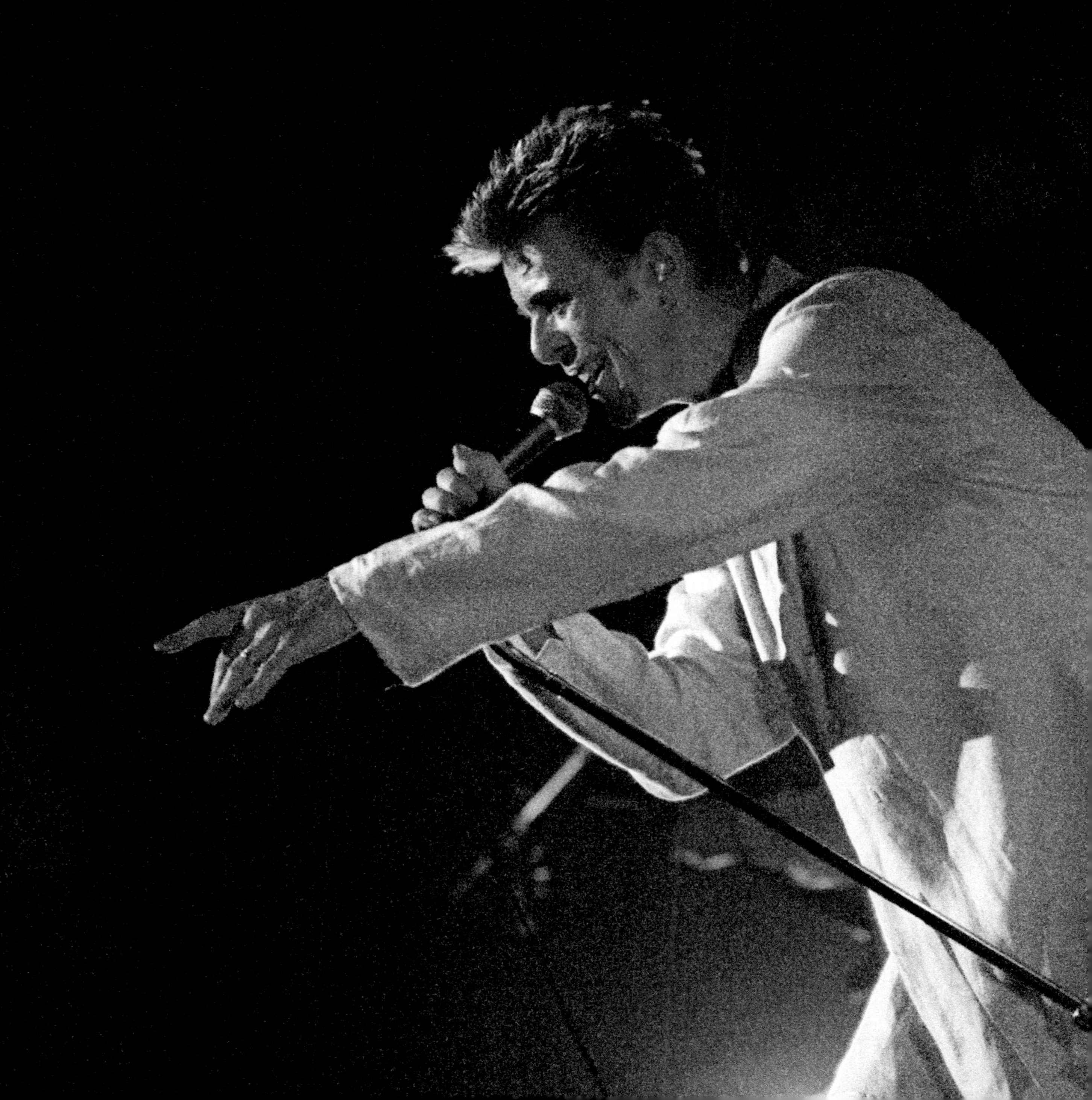

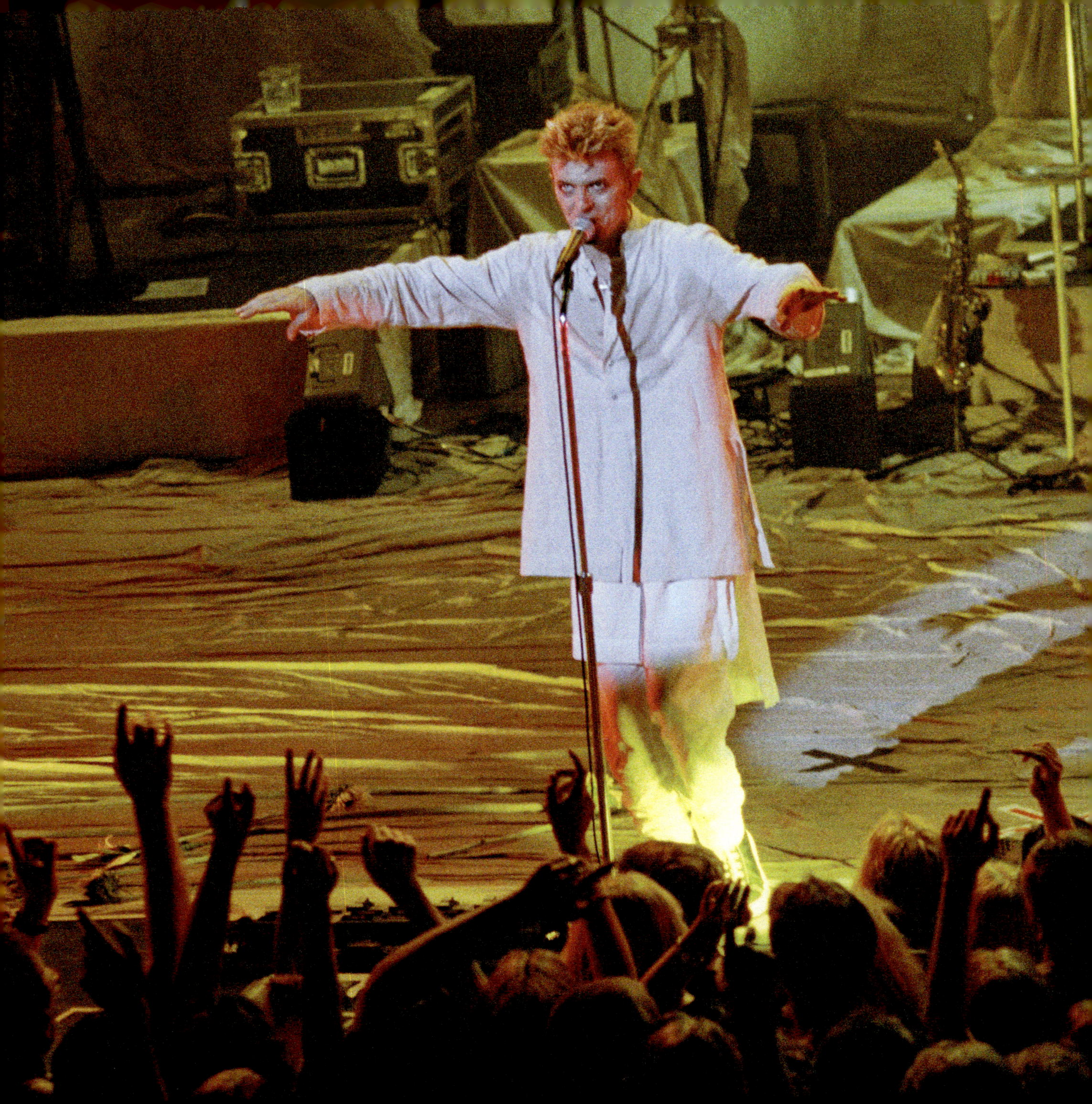

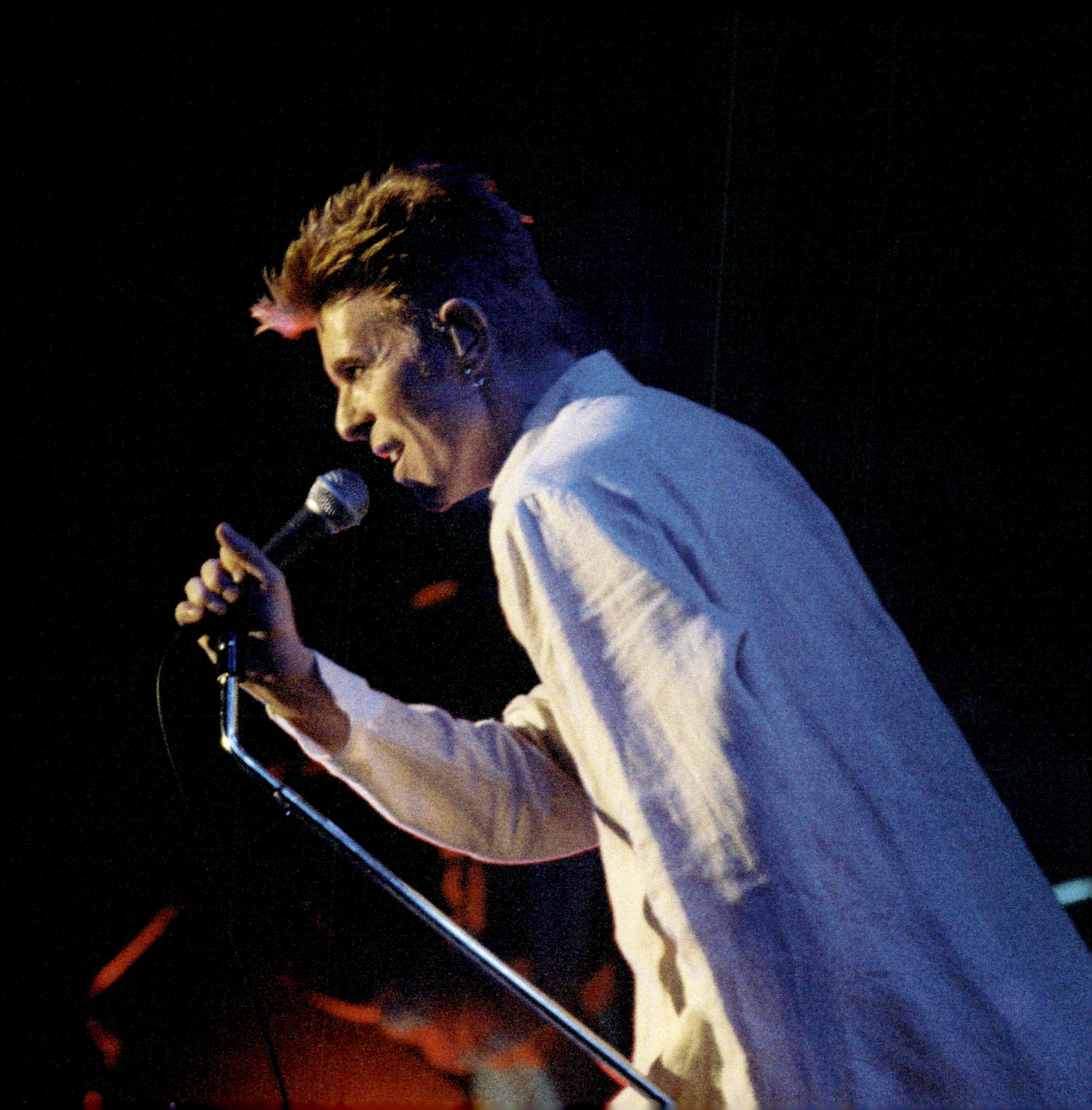

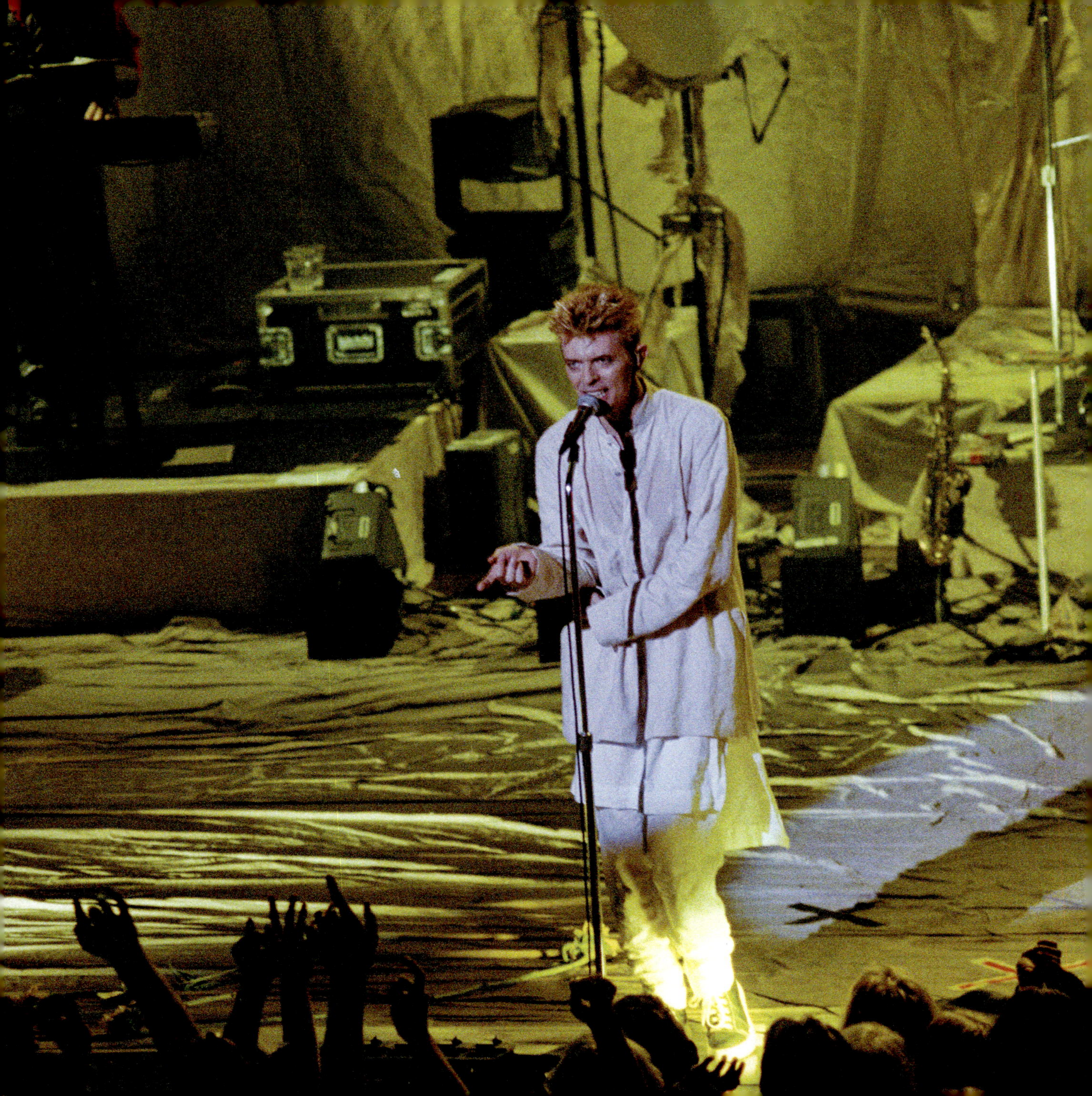

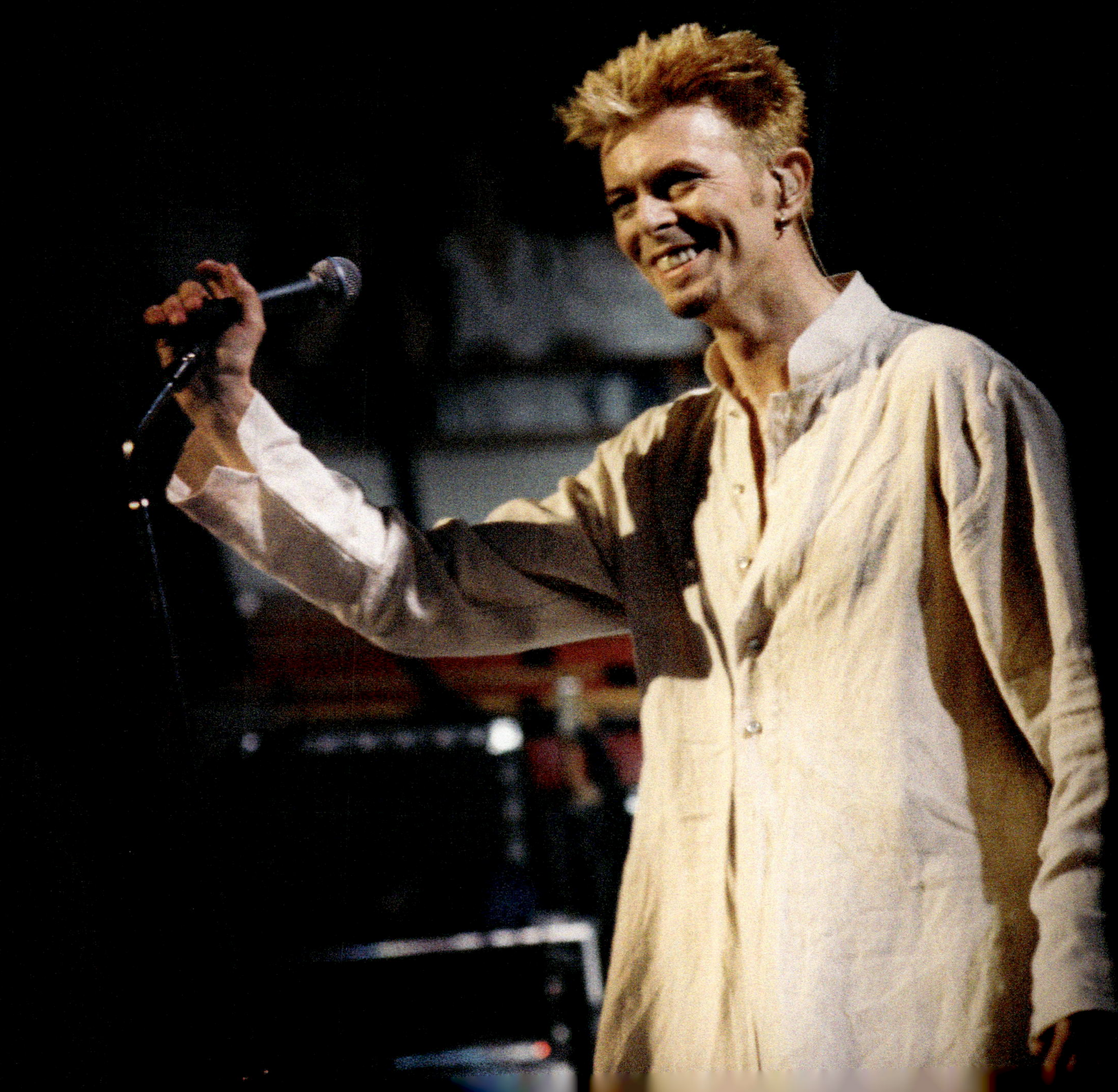

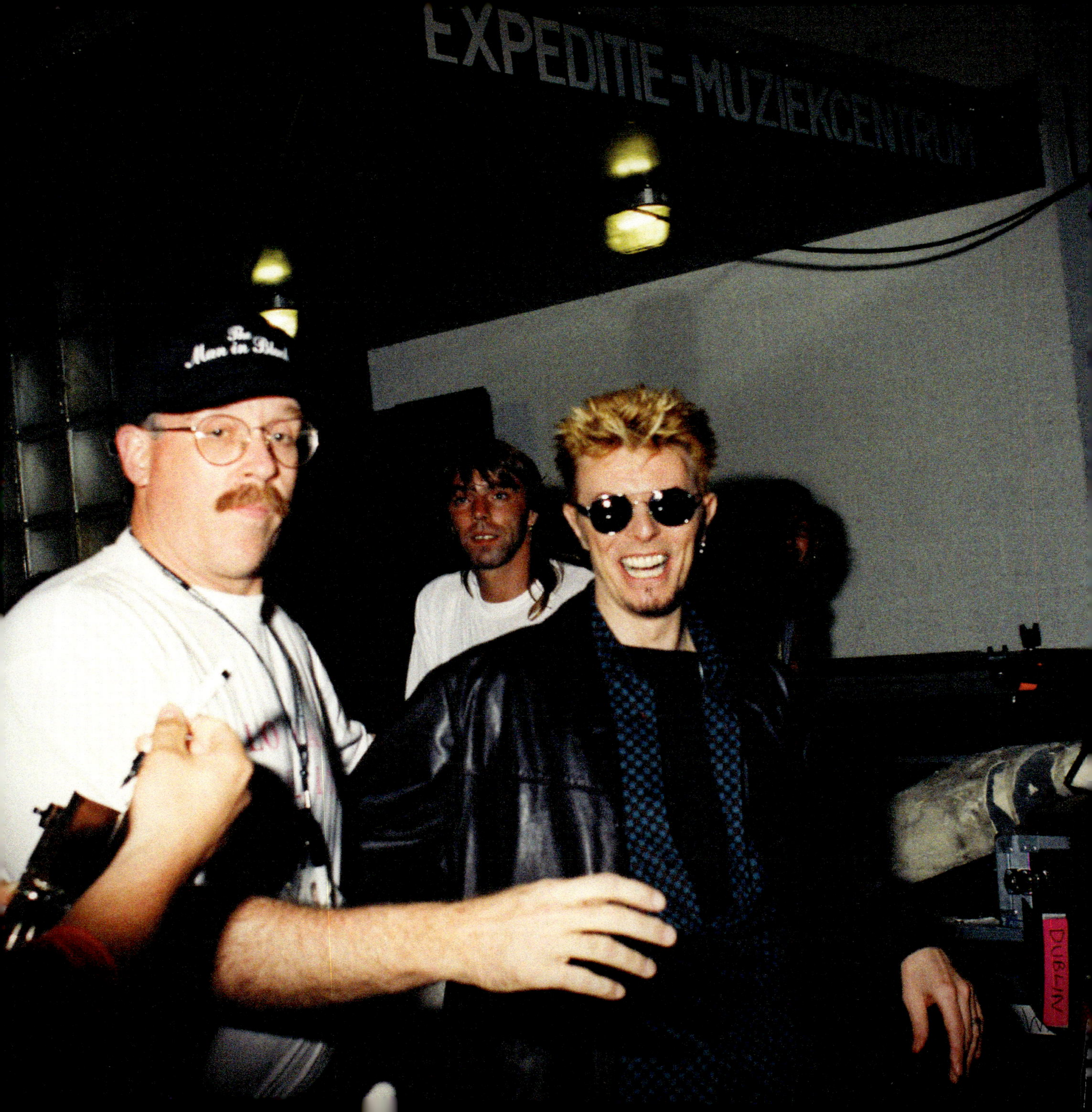
EXPEDITIE - MUZIEKCENTRUM
The Man in Black
DUBLIN

Tour list:

. 30 March 1987, Glass Spider Tour press conference, Paradiso Amsterdam

. 30 May 1987, Glass Spider Tour, Stadion Feijenoord Rotterdam

. 30 March 1990, Sound and Vision Tour, Sportpaleis Ahoy Rotterdam

. 20 October 1991, Tin Machine - It's My Life Tour, Muziekcentrum Vredenburg Utrecht

. 28 January 1996, Outside Tour, Prins van Oranjehal Utrecht

. 16 July 1996, Outside Summer Festivals Tour, Sportpaleis Ahoy Rotterdam

. 11 June 1997, Earthling Tour, Muziekcentrum Vredenburg Utrecht

DAVID BOWIE

ON STAGE IN HOLLAND

THE DUTCH CONCERTS 1987 - 1997
PICTURED BY BERNARD RÜBSAMEN